What Is True Love!

"The cure for divorce"

Gabriel Unaji

What is True Love!

No part of this book may be reproduced, distributed, or transmitted in any form or by any means, including photocopying, recording, or other electronic or mechanical methods, without the prior written permission of the publisher.

ISBN 978-1-5136-5102-6

droftruelove@gmail.com
Gabriel Unaji

Cover Design: Adeola Disu {United Kingdom}
All Scriptural quotations were written from the New International Version except otherwise stated.

Dedication

I dedicate this book to every woman as men will no more have an excuse for not knowing what truelove is, but they will have this book and with the knowledge they gain from it, help every other man in their lives to know and give true love to women.

-Dr. of truelove

Table of Content

Introduction

There are two kinds of ignorance in the world. The first kind has to do with having incorrect knowledge of something while the second one involves having no knowledge at all. The first kind of ignorance is the more dangerous one because when you have incorrect knowledge of something you often do not know and assume that you already know that thing. The result of such perverted knowledge is abuse and misuse of that thing. Our world is suffering from a gross ignorance of one of the greatest gift that humanity has been given. That is the gift of love. Although the word 'Love' is a very popular and commonly used word in the English language, it is also one of the most abused and confused word in its application for daily living. Today, marriages are falling apart and relationships are breaking in pieces. The reason for these menace is not far-fetched; it is linked to our perverted knowledge of what love really means.

The world is in gross ignorance of the true meaning of love and knows only a perverted version of it called human love. Meanwhile love which is true is from above, divine and pure by its nature.

A proper understanding of true love will help us become outstanding in any relationship we find ourselves – whether with family, friends, work colleagues and most especially marriage. In this book, you will learn about the characteristics that define true love and how you can apply them to your marriage, relationship and everyday living. You will learn not to fall in love, but to WALK in love, how to build long lasting marriage and relationship and how to enjoy peace and joy throughout your life's journey. Welcome on board as you come with me on a journey to discovering the only love that is pure, sacrificial and never fails.

See you at the top!

Chapter One

I Love You: the World's Most Used Cliché

Chapter One
I Love You: the World's Most Used Cliché

The words 'I love you' have become one of the most used cliché in the world today. We hear it at home, in schools, at the market places and in restaurants. It is almost impossible to watch a Hollywood movie and not hear the words 'I love you'. R&B music would have no appeal to the world and in fact, remain unpopular if its lyrics is not littered with the words 'I love you'. Teenagers in high school use the word 'love' almost every day as they express how they feel about an opposite sex. Young men in the universities are fond of using the words 'I love you' whenever they are trying to woo a young lady into a relationship with them. We hear married couples recite the words 'I love you' every day to each other. Almost every phone call between two opposite sexes that are emotionally attracted to each other ends with the very same words 'I love you'.

Married couples often ends a quarrel with the words 'I love you' alongside with a session of romance. Pastors preach about love, Imams talk about love and even atheists canvass for love. Love is such a popular word that one would have to be deaf to not have heard it or be blind to not have seen it written somewhere before. Even children have been taught to use the words 'I love you even though they have not the slightest idea of its true meaning. Surprisingly, it is not only children, who are void of the understanding of the true meaning of love. Many adults be it Hollywood stars, secular music artists, Pastors, Christians, Muslims, Atheists, Married couples, university students etc. also have only little or no understanding of the true meaning of the word 'love'. Not only is the world void of the understanding of the true meaning of love but also of its purpose. Majority of the people who use the words 'I love you' do not really understand what they are saying or the purpose of love.

It is a known fact that when the purpose of a thing is not known, its abuse becomes inevitable. Hence we live in a world that chants 'I love you' every day and yet for lack of proper understanding abuse that same love they so much talk about.

The evidence that the world does not know the true meaning of love is seen in the alarming rate of divorce, ethnic and religious crisis, theft, armed robbery, wars, hatred, malice and murder that have become part of our day to day life on this planet called earth. It is for this reason that I have written this book, to bring many people to the understanding of the meaning and purpose of true love. What then is true love?

What True Love Is Not

As we have already discussed, you will agree with me that the word love is one of the most important and widely used words in the English language, but at the same time, it is one of the most misunderstood words.

There is a saying, "Love makes the world go round." But love will only make the world go round if people really understand what true love is. You become outstanding only in what you understand.

Ignorance is the greatest enemy of true love. Based on my knowledge, wisdom and personal experience as a husband and a father, I will define true love in this book using 15 characteristics that embodies the true meaning of the word 'love'

You will discover true love and learn about the characteristics or seeds that keep it alive. By planting these fifteen seeds of true love (characters of true love) as the firm foundation upon which you build your marriage and any meaningful relationships, you would realize that your marriage and relationship will never fail.

However, before I tell you what true love is, I would like to first tell you what it is not.

Every relationship and marriage usually begins with the sweet words 'I love you' and most ends up in divorce with the painful words 'I thought he loved me or I thought she loved me'. This is often the case with not only Hollywood stars and people who are not born again but also with highly devoted Christians and religious leaders. We live in a dispensation in which the rate of divorce among Christian couples is in competition with that of the secular world. If there is so much divorce in the world today among people who once said repeatedly to each other 'I love you', does that not tell us something! Does it not reveal to us that the world lacks the knowledge of what love really is! It is alarming to find that several marriages have been built on what love is not than on true love itself. Most couples and young adults build their relationship and marriage on what they think was love only to get to the end of the road to realize that what they thought was love was mere feelings. They realize no sooner than they start living together in the same house that divorce is inevitable. Until we know what true love is, we would never be able to tell the difference between true love and 'seeming love'

'Seeming love' often looks like true love and tries to mimic it. However, its very nature exposes it for what it is. Below is a description of the nature of 'seeming love'

- It starts and ends spontaneously
- It begins with a feeling of love and ends with a strong hatred for the other person.
- It makes empty and unrealistic promises to the other person
- It is built on emotions and void of logical reasoning.
- It is highly conditional and short-lived

True love doesn't happen right away; it's an ever-growing process. It develops after you've gone through many ups and downs, when you've suffered together, cried together, laughed together. -Ricardo Montalban

The first thing you must know about true love is that it does not happen right away. It is not spontaneous. It is true that as humans we are easily enticed by beauty and outward facades. However, you will be making a mistake to think that you love someone just because you are attracted to his or her facial beauty, height, body shape and size. True love is not spontaneous. It takes time. True love is not the attraction that you have for that woman because of her beauty or for that slim man because of his physique.

True love is beyond mere attraction. Any relationship built on mere attraction is standing on 'seeming love' and is bound to fail eventually. Furthermore, true love is not just a feeling or a hormonal surge that gets us excited when we see the opposite sex. That strong feeling that overwhelms you when you see a beautiful woman or a handsome man is not a marker of true love because often times those feelings die with time, they disappear before you know it.

Most people have started relationships and gone into marriage because of strong feelings only to discover after marriage that those feelings did not even last a year further. That is a proof that it merely seemed like love but not true love in itself. Remember that 'seeming love' often try to mimic true love. It pretends to be true love but it is mere feelings. It begins with a strong feeling of love and ends with a strong hatred for the other person. Many couples who end up having a divorce do so only after realizing that what they thought was true love was mere feelings and hormone-mediated passion. No matter how long we ignorantly try to keep a relationship that is built on 'seeming love' it will eventually crumble. That kind of love will reveal itself for what it is in the end. If it is not true love, it cannot be true love.

True love cannot be found where it does not exist, nor can it be denied where it does.
-Torquato Tasso

Any love that makes empty and unrealistic promises to the other person is definitely not true love. That kind of love is built on emotions and void of logical reasoning. Because it is hormonally -induced, it does not give place for logical reasoning. That is why most men promise their fiancées heaven and earth even though a little reasoning would have shown them that they could not fulfill those promises. Their emotions becloud their sense of reasoning. They are carried away by external qualities that appeal to the eyes. True love on the other hand is logical and thinks through everything to arrive at the best decision.

True love is not a strong, fiery, impetuous passion. It is, on the contrary, an element calm and deep. It looks beyond mere externals, and is attracted by qualities alone. It is wise and discriminating, and its devotion is real and abiding.
-Ellen G. White.

The next time you are in a hurry to say I Love You and make unrealistic promises to the opposite sex, ask yourself if you have thoroughly thought about what you are about to do and if you are making an informed decision. That way, you would calm down and search your heart and medulla Oblongata if they are saying the same thing. When what your heart is saying is different from what your brain is saying, it is better to listen to your brain, the center of logical reasoning. True love is calm and deep, it is wise and discriminates; it always makes the right decisions.

When your partner tells you he or she loves you because of your beauty, your height, your skin color, your body shape or your intonation etc., be rest assured that he or she is void of true love. True love is unconditional but seeming love is mostly conditional. The conditional nature of seeming love makes it short-lived. As soon as those qualities or conditions are no more, that love ends. Most people begin relationships and marriage based on conditions, which often are temporary unknowingly to them. Men are often more guilty of this mistake than women. Most Men marry women because of facial beauty or skin color and texture. They often forget that beauty fades and that human skin does not remain spotless and glossy forever. Reality dawns on them when they notice that after one or two children, their wives no longer look as beautiful as they used to be. Dislike and hatred gradually sets in because the very condition for which they got married is fading before their eyes. It is at this point that unnecessary anger and quarrels become part of the home. Most men also start cheating on their wives at this point. One thing leads to another and divorce is often the end-result. Any relationship built on seeming love will always be short-lived because the conditions that engineered the relationship at the beginning will not always be there. However, for true love it is not short-lived, it is eternal. *If we have built on the fragile cornerstones of human wisdom, pride, and conditional love, things may look good for a while, but a weak foundation causes collapse when storms hit. -Charles Stanley*

"Love is blind" How True?

Hello friend, we have been discussing what true love is not as a preparation to the unveiling of what true love is. I will show you with practical examples what true love really means in the following chapters. However, I would like us to examine the popular saying "Love is blind" to ascertain how true or false it is. This is a crucial step to take if we would understand the nature of true love.

Have you ever heard people say love is blind? I guess you have. What comes to your mind when you hear people make such comments? The proverb love is blind means that loving someone makes you unable to see their faults. As good as that definition may seem I will however like you to know that it is not completely true. Most people have gone into marriage and relationship believing such a half-truth only to discover that they were wrong. To believe that love is blind is to become delusional and allow emotions blind us. If you get married to someone believing that you will never see their faults because you love them, you will be surprised to find that true love sees. If you are not married, you may want to ask married couples if love sees or not. If they are honest with you, they will tell you that true love sees. True love is not blind; it sees the fault of the other person and loves them all the same. Seeming love on the other hand claims to be blind during courtship and when it begins to see the fault of a partner in marriage, it is dumbfounded and taken aback.

Because it was not prepared for what it sees, handling it becomes difficult. The outcome of such unpreparedness is anger, frustration, quarrels and in most cases divorce.

However, for true love, it is always prepared and well aware that everyone has some faults and weaknesses but chooses to love in spite of them. True love sees your faults and despite them loves you. One of the secrets to a lasting marriage is to love the other person despite their faults. True love says, "even though I see your faults and weaknesses, I love you all the same".

Love is not "If" or "Because." Love is "anyway", "even though" and "in spite of"

Nuggets

1. The evidence that the world does not know the true meaning of love is seen in the alarming rate of divorce, ethnic and religious crisis, theft, armed robbery, wars, hatred, malice and murder that have become part of our day to day life on this planet called earth.

2. Every relationship and marriage usually begins with the sweet words 'I love you' and most ends up in divorce with the painful words 'I thought he loved me or I thought she loved me'.

3. If there is so much divorce in the world today among people who once said repeatedly to each other 'I love you', does that not tell us something! Does it not reveal to us that the world lacks the knowledge of what love really is

4. True love is beyond mere attraction. Any relationship built on mere attraction is standing on 'seeming love' and is bound to fail eventually

5. It is true that as humans we are easily enticed by beauty and outward facades. However, you will be making a mistake to think that you love someone just because you are attracted to his or her facial beauty, height, body shape and size. True love is not spontaneous.

6. When what your heart is saying is different from what your brain is saying, it is better to listen to your brain, the center of logical reasoning. True love is calm and deep, it is wise and discriminates; it always makes the right decisions.

7. Any relationship built on seeming love will always be short-lived because the

conditions that engineered the relationship at the beginning will not always be there. However, for true love it is not short-lived, it is eternal.

8. If you get married to someone believing that you will never see their faults because you love them, you will be surprised to find that true love sees.

9. True love sees your faults and despite them loves you. One of the secrets to a lasting marriage is to love the other person despite their faults.

10. One of the secrets to a lasting marriage is to love the other person despite their faults. True love says, "even though I see your faults and weaknesses, I love you all the same".

Chapter Two

Understanding the Types of Love

Chapter Two
Understanding the Types of Love

We live in a world in which people use the word 'love' every day to express how they feel about something or someone. However, not too many persons know or understand that there are different kinds of love with each having its own meaning. This lack of understanding of the types of love and their meanings is the reason there is so much abuse of the word 'love'. The relationship crisis and divorce that is prevalent in our societies today are linked to nothing more than our ignorance of the types and meaning of love. If we must build healthy and long-lasting relationships, we must educate ourselves on the meaning and types of love; we must come to the full understanding of the meaning of love.

In order for us to, fully understand, what love is and become outstanding in our knowledge of true love, we need to know the four kinds of love from the Greek Language.

Eros- Romantic & Sexual Love

The first kind of love that we need to discuss is EROS – this is the romantic or sexual love. It is the most common type of love that we see in Hollywood movies and perhaps the only type of love that everyone expresses unconsciously. Without being taught or instructed, everyone grows up to realize that he or she is sexually attracted to the opposite sex. This kind of love is natural and controlled by the physical senses. Hence, Eros love is physical love. This kind of love usually physically and passionately attracts people to the opposite sex. Although we all naturally feel this erotic love, yet many people especially Christians demonize it or try to shy away from talking about it. Moreover, because everyone shies away from talking about it, teenagers and young adults are left in ignorance of what this Eros love really means. They only realize that they are burning with passion for the opposite gender and have a natural desire to have sex but they do not know how to handle or manage this consuming passion.

A lot of the unwanted pregnancies and abortions that we see among young people in our secondary schools and universities could have been prevented if parents explained to their children the nature of Eros love and how they can manage it.

Unfortunately, most parents themselves do not even know the difference between true love and Eros love. Majority of married couples in our present world got married because they were overwhelmed by a burning desire to have romance and sex with the partner with whom they were accustomed. Many thought that what they felt for each other was true love and did not know that it was mere Eros love. They discover only some years after marriage that the burning desire and attraction to the opposite sex is not the definition of true love. While it is true that Eros love is not the true love, we must not make the mistake of demonizing it.

We should rather learn how to manage it and identify it for what it is. What if I told you that Eros love is not satanic and that God himself created it! In fact, this type of love existed before the fall of man, before sin came into the world. When Adam, the first man saw Eve, the first woman for the first time, he felt a physical and romantic attraction towards her.

21And the Lord God caused a deep sleep to fall on Adam, and he slept; and He took one of his ribs, and closed up the flesh in its place. 22Then the rib which the Lord God had taken from man He made into a woman, and He brought her to the man. 23And Adam said: "This is now bone of my bones and flesh of my flesh; she shall be called Woman, because she was taken out of Man." 24Therefore a man shall leave his father and mother and be joined to his wife, and they shall become one flesh. 25And they were both naked, the man and his wife, and were not ashamed. {Genesis 2:21-25}

From the verses above, we see that Adam was attracted to his wife Eve and identified her as bone of his bone and flesh of his flesh. Immediately after that the next thing we see the writer say is *"Therefore a man shall leave his father and mother and be joined to his wife, and they shall become one flesh"*. What does this mean? It means that a man will always be attracted to a woman and the result of that attraction is leaving father and mother to cleave or join to the other partner, the woman. Two chapters after the event we read above, the bible recorded that Adam knew or had sexual intercourse with his wife and they bore a son called Cain. What does that tell us? It tells us that sexual attraction to the opposite sex has always been from the beginning. Therefore, romantic love or Eros was created by God to attract us to the opposite sex but God's intention is for us to express that love only within the confines of marriage as it was with Adam and Eve.

However, it is important to note that Eros is not the true love that keeps a marriage together. While Romantic love or Eros attracts us to our partners, it does not have what it takes to keep a marriage together. The numerous amounts of divorce cases in our society are a proof that Eros alone cannot keep a marriage. We need something more than Eros, called True Love to be able to maintain healthy and long-lasting relationships.

The romantic love we feel toward the opposite sex is probably one extra help from God to bring you together, but that's it. All the rest of it, the true love, is the test.

-Joan Chen

The reason relationships fail often times is that most people know only romantic love but not true love. If all you know is only romantic or natural love, you will not be able to give true love to your partner.

This physical love (sex) is the fastest way to know if a man or woman has truelove or only natural love. The man with truelove will have patience but the man with only natural love (lust) is always in a hurry for sex. Such a man is all about sex and the moment he has sex with the opposite sex, that is it, he is done with her! She becomes a statistics.

 When next the woman calls him and asks him "why can't you give me love?" he replies "I made love to you when we met, so what do you want from me". He tells her 'I made love to you because that is what I have'. She is asking him for genuine love, but he does not have that, so he made the one he has 'sex' (physical love). A man can only give you what he has, not what he does not have. The woman not feeling fulfilled and being starved of genuine love, walks away and the relationship ends.

What has happened? The man has expressed his Eros outside of marriage thinking that it would keep them together in relationship, but the exact opposite happened. Eros destroyed the relationship! It is often the case that when Eros is expressed outside the confines of marriage, it leads to resentment, low self-esteem, anger and eventual repudiation. That is why Eros love is best expressed within marriage; only to your wife or husband. Any expression of Eros outside marriage leads to disaster in the end. Men and women without sexual control end up destroying their homes. This happens in homes where there are no foundations of true love.

Phileo –Brotherly and Friendship Love

The second kind of love we need to understand is the Phileo kind of love. This is the warm love among friends. This kind of warm, close and brotherly love can result from friendship developed from school, work place, social events, in sports and so on.

This happens when best of friends show great affection towards one another all based on feelings. This is not true love because it is based on feelings and feelings come and go, but when both friends have truelove, the feelings changes to act of the will.

 So many close friends have done great things for their friends and when they hurt their friends in some ways, the friends found it difficult to forgive them. A good example are ex – convicts who come out of Jails and finds out that their so-called best and close friends have slept with their wives or girlfriends while they were in prison.

This also happens with so-called close friends outside jails who do this to their friends due to pride and competition. We have seen women who happen to be close friends fighting one another, accusing each other of sleeping with their boyfriends or husbands.

While husbands and wives need to express erotic love within marriage, there is need for them to, also express Phileo. Most marriages fail because both partners do not become or live as close friends. In many marriages, the atmosphere within the home is very unfriendly as the couples live like strangers or as masters and slaves. In a house where the husband sees himself as the master and the wife as the slave, it will be difficult to express Phileo to each other. Without Phileo, marriage becomes boring, unhappy and burdensome.

"It is not a lack of love, but a lack of friendship that makes unhappy marriages."
— Friedrich Nietzsche
Most men and women have best friends at their work places whom they share jokes, fears, worries etc. with but relate with their partners at home as strangers.

Husbands and wives are supposed to be best of friends. A man should be able to discuss his fears, worries, and jokes, excitements with his wife and vice versa. They should be able to laugh at each other's mistakes and correct each other in love. Even when erotic love drives them to have sex, they should spice it up with Phileo by playing together, having fun and romance at the same time. Although Phileo is not the true love, it is needed in every marriage to keep a friendly atmosphere and make marriage fun.

Storge – Family Love

The third kind of love you need to know to, fully understand what true love really, means is called Storge. Storge is a kind of natural or instinctual affection, towards members of one's family. Such love exists between parents and their children for example. This kind of love is the love relationship enjoyed by a close-knit family.

It is natural and hence can easily crumble. So many families today are breaking up because of the challenges of life. In ancient times, families used to be much closed. Although storge love is good for keeping families together, yet it is not good enough for making a marriage last.

Only a marriage built on true love can last forever. When marriages were built on truelove, the church played a key role in the societies. However, the situation is different today because only few people go to church. Most of our marriages today are built on natural love. Unfortunately, natural love has no strong foundation to build the family on, so any little challenge, the family love collapses.

The husbands say 'I don't love you anymore or the wives say I am tired of this relationship. However, if the families were built on true love, challenges of life become a stepping-stone. Such families overcome every challenge thrown at them by the evil one. These are families were the husbands' love their wives and the wives understand that they are one with their husbands.

AGAPE –The Highest Form of Love

We have been using the word true love since the beginning of this book. You probably would have wondered what exactly this true love is. Yea! You need to know it. It is called 'agape'. It is the purest and highest form of love. Agape is divine love, it is love as God intended it to be: sacrificial, selfless and everlasting.

True love therefore, is the divine love of God, unnatural and sacrificially expressed in us. It is the willful laying down of one's rights and privileges to satisfy or please the other person. It was such a love that Jesus the Christ modeled for us on the cross when he died for us when we were still sinners.

Agape love is of God and only from God; it is supernatural, not natural as we have in the other three kinds of love. This is what differentiates agape love from the other types of love.

Until we know this Agape love and resolve to live by it in our marriages, relationships and everyday life, we have not known love yet. It does not matter how much of Eros, Phileo, or Storge you have, until you have agape love, you are still void of true love.

Agape love has fifteen characteristics, which we will unveil in the remaining chapters of this book. If there is anything worth searching for, anything worth knowing, anything worth craving, it is the love called Agape. When all is said and done and everything else is no more, Agape love abides forever. Blessed are those whose marriages and relationships stand upon the foundation of Agape love. They will know real joy, peace and everlasting love.

Nuggets

1. The relationship crisis and divorce that is prevalent in our societies today are linked to nothing more than our ignorance of the types and meaning of love.

2. If we must build healthy and long-lasting relationships, we must educate ourselves on the meaning and types of love; we must come to the full understanding of the meaning of love.

3. It is important to note that Eros is not the true love that keeps a marriage together. While Romantic love or Eros attracts us to our partners, it does not have what it takes to keep a marriage together.

4. The numerous amounts of divorce cases in our society are a proof that Eros alone cannot keep a marriage. We need something more than Eros,

called True Love to be able to maintain healthy and long-lasting relationships.

5. The reason relationships fail often times is that most people know only romantic love but not true love. If all you know is only romantic or natural love, you will not be able to give true love to your partner.

6. It is often the case that when Eros is expressed outside the confines of marriage, it leads to resentment, low self-esteem, anger and eventual repudiation. That is why Eros love is best expressed within marriage; only to your wife or husband.

7. Any expression of Eros outside marriage leads to disaster in the end. Men and women without sexual control end up destroying their homes. This happens

in homes where there are no
foundations of true love.

8. In a house where the husband sees
himself as the master and the wife as
the slave, it will be difficult to express
Phileo to each other. Without Phileo,
marriage becomes boring, unhappy
and burdensome.

9. True love is the divine love of God,
unnatural and sacrificially expressed
in us. It is the willful laying down of
one's rights and privileges to satisfy or
please the other person.

10. Agape is the purest and highest form
of love. It is divine love, it is love as
God intended it to be: sacrificial,
selfless and everlasting.

11. Until we know this Agape love and
resolve to live by it in our marriages,
relationships and everyday life, we
have not known love yet. It does not

matter how much of Eros, Phileo, or
Storge you have, until you have agape
love, you are still void of true love.

12. If there is anything worth searching
for, anything worth knowing,
anything worth craving, it is the love
called Agape. When all is said and
done and everything else is no more,
Agape love abides forever. Blessed are
those whose marriages and
relationships stand upon the
foundation of Agape love. They will
know real joy, peace and everlasting
love.

Chapter Three

Love Never Fails

Chapter Three
Love Never Fails

One of the characteristics of true love; the last one among the 15 seeds of true love that you will learn in this book is "love never fails". True love lasts forever. It stands the test of time and it is everlasting.

8 Love never fails. But where there are prophecies, they will cease; where there are tongues, they will be stilled; where there is knowledge, it will pass away.
(1 Corinthians 13:8 NIV)

Our world is full of people who say I love you today and hate you the next day. The number of marriages that start and end in divorce in a world that talk so much about love as ours is alarming. You cannot imagine that with the huge number of Hollywood's movies centered on love and romance, marriages still fail so quickly as easy as they do.

From North America to Australia, from South America to Africa and from Europe to Asia the situation is the same; marriages fail as quickly as they begin. The reason of course is not far-fetched. The world has a distorted view of love. It neither knows what true love is nor understands its characteristics. The movies and the magazines have painted an unrealistic picture of love to the masses and many people have believed a lie unknowingly to them. People have been told how to fall in love easily yet without the knowledge of what true love really is. Phileo and Eros have taken center stage while little or nothing is known about Agape. I am not appalled at all at the rate at which marriages fail. When the purpose of a thing is not known, it will definitely be abused.

Until the world understands the eternal, sacrificial and selfless nature of true love, people will keep falling in love and falling apart.

Fall In Love and Fall Apart

I cannot really pinpoint the exact moment when everything began to fall apart, but I want to say it started while we were registering for our wedding in china. I remember that day as if it was yesterday, standing in the middle of Macy's arguing over which plates we would scan with that stupid gun. He wanted something plain and unassuming. I was leaning toward patterns and colors. I thought we were just succumbing to the stress of wedding planning. All couples fight during this process; at least, that is what the magazines all said. However, those plates were a metaphor for our entire relationship. We were fundamentally two very different people. Unfortunately, we figured it out four months too late.

I should have called our wedding off a dozen times leading up to the "I do's," but I did not. I just kept pushing forward because I believed the lie the bridal magazines had sold me: that it would all get easier after the stress of wedding planning was over. We just had to get through that one day and we would have our entire lives to get back on track.

"Let's just get this over with" is not the mantra you want to be repeating as you walk down the aisle, but it is the tune that played in my head as my father gave me away.

In a fitting start to our lives as husband and wife, it rained almost every day of our honeymoon. We were wet and uncomfortable when we found ourselves arguing over plates again in a small Mexican gift shop. I had fallen in love with the bold colors and Aztec prints that surrounded us during our stay in Mexico, but he seemed to want to keep our home devoid of color.

The fighting continued on the flight home and into the first few weeks of our marriage. Instead of celebrating our newfound freedom from wedding planning, we began to look for freedom from one another.

One month after our wedding, I sat alone in our bed eating sushi, my husband out somewhere else instead of being home with me to eat it. One month after our wedding, alone in our bed, I Googled, "marriage counselors in our area" and "how do I get an annulment?"

We spent the next month searching for the silver bullet that would save our marriage. He offered to stop going out to the bar every night with his single brothers. I promised to do more fun things and spend less time at work. We would make an effort for a bit but then fall right back into our old habits.

Then we would cry, fight, and cry some more while asking each other how we got to this point. I finally made an appointment with a marriage counselor, but the day before we were scheduled to see her, he called me while I was walking into my office.

"I'm not even sure I want this marriage to work," he confessed. I knew what he meant. The stupid plates that we had fought over sat unopened in our spare bedroom. How could our marriage be over before we would even put away the gifts? There were still bits of wrapping paper stuck with Scotch tape on the side of one of the boxes. I noticed it as he walked through our living room with them on the day he moved out.

My mother took me to meet with the divorce attorney. He was a kind man who quietly slid a box of tissues across his desk when I began to cry. My mother also took me to a bar on the way home. We sat there at 2 p.m. on a Tuesday afternoon, and she quietly slid an ice-cold beer into my hand when I began to cry.

I had never been more miserable in my life than I was in the year leading up to that afternoon in the bar, but the end of my marriage was never the solution that I had hoped for. I just wished we had never gotten married in the first place.

It wasn't long before I got angry. I felt tricked into marrying a man who had no intentions of remaining married to me. I imagined him as a time thief, having robbed me of both the past few years and the years to come.

Waves of guilt would hit me as well. What could I have done differently? Where did I go wrong? Should I have changed for him? Should I have changed for his family that never thought I was good enough?

Eventually, I would discover the full truth of the matter, which involved an overdrawn checking account and other women. My guilt shifted slightly from blaming myself for the failure of our marriage to wondering why I had not been able to see that it had been doomed all along. My anger returned; was I blind or just stupid?

The days and weeks following the divorce from my husband of four months were full of sadness and embarrassment. I hid away in my house until enough time had passed that I assumed the news was public knowledge.

The sadness came and went. As time went on, I realized that I was mourning something that never really existed. The man I had fallen in love with and agreed to marry was not the same man I said, "I do" to. I grieved the loss of that life almost as much as I grieved for what I expected to be my tainted future.

I was surprised by the variety and strength of these emotions, but the biggest shock of all ended up being how quickly life went back to normal. One day I was sitting alone on my couch crying over diaper commercials and the next I was laughing in the middle of the mall with my sister. It was as if the past few months had happened to somebody else.

It was on one of those perfectly normal nights, five months and two weeks after my wedding day, that I met the actual love of my life. He never cared that I was an almost-30-year-old divorcee with a few cats. He never minded that I was gun-shy and had no interest in anything more than some casual fun. He didn't want me to change; he liked who I was. Five years and seven months after that fateful wedding day, I walked down the aisle again. We are still very happy with our plates, a teal and white set we got from Target, and every night we use them to eat dinner with our two daughters. In the end, I would not change anything that happened, because it all brought me here and here is where I was always meant to be.[1]

 (Story as told by Lauren Wellbank, a writer, blogger and mother.)

When people fall in love, they are likely to fall out of it sooner than they envisage. The reason is that the "in love feeling" that most people talk about is often a characteristics of Eros love not that of true love. Most people often misinterpret that feeling of romance, sex and passion that usually overwhelms us when we are attracted to the opposite gender for the first time as true love. Unfortunately, the feelings do not last forever. They come and go. They are short-lived and do not last long. Hormones in our body chemically initiate such feelings and we erroneously interpret them as "falling in love". If you fall too soon in love, you will fall out of love just as quickly as you fell in. That was the case with Lauren Wellbank, whose story you read above; she had fallen in love with a man she thought truly loved her only to discover that true love is not defined by mere feelings but by real and genuine characteristics.

The 'in love feeling' that she had initially soon turned sour. Pain, arguments, crying, quarrels and misery soon became her reality. Wanting to pretend about how she felt, she decided to go ahead with their marriage plans. To her greatest surprise, falling in love is far different from real Agape love. They could only manage to tolerate each other for about four months before they had a divorce. They fell in love, married and fell apart barely four months after the marriage. What a tragedy! Lauren's case is one of many such cases of people falling in love and falling apart. The reason of course is not far-fetched; human love, natural or Eros love is transient. Only true love is eternal, unending and everlasting.

Many Waters Cannot Quench Love

When Solomon the King wrote in his songs the following words *"Many waters cannot quench love, nor can the floods drown it.*

If a man would give for love all the wealth of his house, it would be utterly despised" he was revealing one of the greatest secrets to a lasting marriage and relationship. I believe that he was inspired to expose perhaps the greatest characteristics of true love; i.e. love is eternal. When he said 'many waters cannot quench love, nor can the floods drown it', he was invariably saying that love would overcome all obstacles and challenges and last forever. Yes! True love will last forever. Nothing can overcome it! If a love cannot stand the test of time, then it is not true love. If a love blossoms only in good times and dies in the face of misunderstandings, it was never true love.

Most people make the mistake of concluding too early that what they feel for the other person or vice versa is true love before such love had been tested. That is why most young people who are consumed by Erotic passion conclude that they are in love and hurriedly get married only to discover sooner than they would expect that they had made a mistake. Love must pass through many waters (troubles, misunderstandings, disagreements, quarrels) and still blossom before we could call it true love. For most people this time of testing happens in the first few years of marriage. That is the time when the other person's weaknesses and faults that you never noticed during those years of feeling and falling in love becomes glaring.

The love that you claimed was blind suddenly receives its sight and focuses strangely more on your partner's shortfalls, excesses and flaws. You are then tempted to believe that you made a wrong choice and if given another chance would choose someone else whom you perceive from afar to be perfect. Hatred, disgust, unnecessary arguments and fights becomes the routine in your home and if you do not take care, one of you would be heading to court to file for a divorce.

One of the questions that comes to mind at such times is "Why me? Why is this happening to me?" Well, to be frank with you, it is not just about you; all humans go through such testing times. Almost every marriage goes through the same waters that come to test the strength of our love.

13 No temptation has overtaken you except such as is common to man; but God is faithful, who will not allow you to be tempted beyond what you are able, but with the temptation will also make the way of escape, that you may be able to bear it. (1 Corinthians 10:13)

The eternal nature of true love makes it possible for us to overcome the test. If what you have is true love many waters cannot quench it, floods cannot drown it. True love will stand the test of time. It will overcome the challenges and the hurdles and blossom forever. This is why I desire that every couple understand what true love is and express it in their marriages. The ease with which people fall in and out of love in our societies today is a proof that most people lack the eternal, everlasting love called Agape. The increasing statistics of divorce rate is an evidence of how void of true love our world is. It does not matter how often love is talked about in the media, in movies and in romantic songs, until we know the true unfailing Agape love; we have not known love at all. The only type of love that never fails, the only one that hold marriages together "till death do you part" is Agape love.

Men and women with agape love never divorce their wives or husbands, but men and women without agape love divorce easily with very flimsy excuses. If it is true love, it will last forever, for love in its purest form is eternal.

I have Loved You with an Everlasting Love

Every man who desires to enjoy a lasting marriage must come to a point in his life where he can say to his wife "I have loved you with an everlasting love" and beyond just saying it, mean it. True love, which is Agape, is from God and manifests itself in us in the same fashion as God expresses it. Many years ago, scriptures recorded that the God of the universe appeared to the Jewish Prophet Jeremiah and said to him the following words: *"Yes, I have loved you with an everlasting love; Therefore with loving-kindness I have drawn you."*
{Jeremiah 31:3b}

This is Agape love in display. Men should express this kind of love to their wives if their marriages must last. I know most men will find it difficult to come to such a height of love that says 'I have you loved with an everlasting love'. Although many would say it during courtship and in the first few months after marriage, most would not dare say it after some years in marriage. The reason is that they cannot seem to understand why they should promise a woman who perhaps has some flaws, weaknesses and faults everlasting love. Many men would say 'she is stubborn, she does not submit to me, she is this and she is that, I don't think I can promise her such a love'. Well, they say that because they do not understand what true love really means. They do not know that true love loves forever even if the other partner does not deserve it. When God told Jeremiah that he has everlasting love for him, it was not because the prophet was without fault. God had factored in his flaws, weaknesses and faults while making that statement. If your love is true, it would love

beyond all faults. Let's see how God demonstrated this Agape love to Israel:
"For a mere moment I have forsaken you, but with great mercies I will gather you. 8 With a little wrath I hid my face from you for a moment; but with everlasting kindness I will have mercy on you," Says the Lord, your Redeemer. 9 "For this is like the waters of Noah to Me; For as I have sworn That the waters of Noah would no longer cover the earth, So have I sworn That I would not be angry with you, nor rebuke you. 10 For the mountains shall depart and the hills be removed, But My kindness shall not depart from you, nor shall my covenant of peace be removed," Says the Lord, who has mercy on you.
{Isaiah 54:7-10}

From the verses above, we see how God related with Israel when they misbehaved; he was angry with them for a moment and forsook them for a moment, but because Agape love is forever, God could not cast them off forever or divorce them forever. With that everlasting love he had mercy on them and took an oath never to be angry at them again. God swore that his everlasting love will never depart from them again. That is true love. That is how couples are supposed to relate with each other. In every marriage, there will sometimes be misunderstandings. Couples sometimes get angry at each other, but the unfortunate thing is that not many couples know how to express Agape love. Hence, anger leads to malice, malice leads to hatred and hatred leads to divorce. However, for God, the opposite is true; his anger is for a moment and his loving kindness and mercy soon replaces that anger. The result is everlasting love and togetherness. You and I must learn to love like God loves if we must have lasting marriages and relationships. We

must give mercy instead of judgment,
everlasting love instead of everlasting wrath
and a covenant of peace and togetherness
instead of war and divorce. The man who
loves like God loves will enjoy a heaven-on-
earth marriage. He will testify that truly, love
is eternal, many waters cannot quench it.
*True love is eternal, infinite, and always like
itself. It is equal and pure, without violent
demonstrations: it is seen with white hairs
and is always young in the heart.*
-Honore de Balzac

Nuggets

1. The world has a distorted view of love. It neither knows what true love is nor understands its characteristics.

2. People have been told how to fall in love easily yet without the knowledge of what true love really is. Phileo and Eros have taken center stage while little or nothing is known about Agape.

3. Until the world understands the eternal, sacrificial and selfless nature of true love, people will keep falling in love and falling apart.

4. When people fall in love, they are likely to fall out of it sooner than they envisage. The reason is that the "in love feeling" that most people talk about is often a characteristics of Eros love not that of true love.

5. Most people often misinterpret that feeling of romance, sex and passion that usually overwhelms us when we are attracted to the opposite gender for the first time as true love. Unfortunately, the feelings do not last forever. They come and go. They are short-lived and do not last long.

6. Yes! True love will last forever. Nothing can overcome it! If a love cannot stand the test of time, then it is not true love. If a love blossoms only in good times and dies in the face of misunderstandings, it was never true love.

7. Love must pass through many waters (troubles, misunderstandings, disagreements, quarrels) and still blossom before we could call it true love.

8. The eternal nature of true love makes it possible for us to overcome trying times. If what you have is true love many waters cannot quench it, floods cannot drown it. True love will stand the test of time. It will overcome the challenges and the hurdles and blossom forever.

9. The ease with which people fall in and out of love in our societies today is a proof that most people lack the eternal, everlasting love called Agape. The increasing statistics of divorce rate is an evidence of how void of true love our world is.

10. It does not matter how often love is talked about in the media, in movies and in romantic songs, until we know the true unfailing Agape love; we have not known love at all.

11. The only type of love that never fails, the only one that hold marriages together "till death do you part" is Agape love.

12. Men and women with agape love never divorce their wives or husbands, but men and women without agape love divorce easily with very flimsy excuses. If it is true love, it will last forever, for love in its purest form is eternal.

13. Every man who desires to enjoy a lasting marriage must come to a point in his life where he can say to his wife "I have loved you with an everlasting love" and beyond just saying it, mean it.

14. You and I must learn to love like God loves if we must have lasting marriages and relationships. We must give mercy instead of judgment,

everlasting love instead of everlasting wrath and a covenant of peace and togetherness instead of war and divorce. The man who loves like God loves will enjoy a heaven-on-earth marriage. He will testify that truly, love is eternal, many waters cannot quench it.

Chapter Four

The DNA of Real Love

Chapter Four
The DNA of Real Love

True love is made up of building blocks in the same fashion as genes are made up of DNA. In this chapter, we shall look at the building blocks of true love and how every man and woman can build a successful marriage using these building blocks of true love.

15 Seeds (characters) of True Love

The building blocks or DNA of true love are the characteristics or traits that define true love. They are the seeds from which true love emanate. Until we plant these seeds in our marriages, we would never be able to enjoy a blissful and peaceful marriage. Marriages fail because couples lack the building blocks or DNA of true Love. The best thing a man can do for himself and his wife is to make sure that their marriage is built upon the DNA of true love. Couples must learn the traits of true love and make a conscious effort to imbibe them and live by them.

How do you feel when you see couples who have been married for over 50years or 60years still in love with each other even at old age? How do you feel when you see an old man and his wife still holding hands, laughing together and embracing each other? Does it bring joy to your heart? Do you wish to grow old with your partner in genuine love and peace forever? The secret is simple: the 15seeds of true love. When you see grey-headed couples expressing love to each other, don't think it was through a miracle that they were able to keep a loving and lasting relationship. No! It wasn't by miracle; it was by following the principles of true love which are the seeds or DNA of true love. True love is built upon the foundation of 15 seeds or characteristics which when expressed have the capacity to keep marriages forever. Whoever builds their love on these seeds will have a long lasting marriage. The reason is that, in life, you reap what you sow; if you plant good seeds, you get good plants with lovely flowers or good fruits, but if you plants bad seeds, you get poor plants and no flowers or fruit.

The foundations you build your marriage or relationships on determine the outcome. If you build on the foundation of truelove, you will have a marriage on the rock and it will never fail. But if you build your marriage on human love (lust), it will fail because you have built on a shallow foundation.

The question however, is where do we find these 15 seeds of true love? We find them in the word of God. God is the author of love and marriage and has given us the blueprint of true love and lasting marriage in his word. I believe you would like your marriage to last forever. Follow me as I begin to teach you how to do it.

4 Love is patient, love is kind. It does not envy, it does not boast, it is not proud. 5 It does not dishonor others, it is not self-seeking, it is not easily angered, it keeps no record of wrongs. 6 Love does not delight in evil but rejoices with the truth. 7 It always protects, always trusts, always hopes, always perseveres. 8 Love never fails. But where there are prophecies, they will cease; where there are tongues, they will be stilled; where there is knowledge, it will pass away.
1 Corinthians 13:4-8(NIV)

From the verses above, we see the 15 seeds or traits of true love. **Truelove**:

1. *Is Patient*
2. *Is Kind*
3. *Does Not Envy*
4. *Does Not Boast*
5. *Is Not Proud*
6. *Is Not Rude*
7. *Is Not Self – Seeking*
8. *Is Not Easily Angered*
9. *Keeps No Records of Wrongs*

10.   *Does Not Delight In Evil, but Rejoices In the Truth*

11.   *Always Protects*

12.   *Always Trusts*

13.   *Always Hopes*

14.   *Always Perseveres*

15. *Never Fails*

Can you just imagine for a minute how your marriage and relationship would be if it were built on the above building blocks! Imagine that you and your partner express these traits in your marriage and relationship. Trust me, your marriage would be heaven-on-earth, your relationship would be blissful and peaceful. Anyone who wants to put an end to the quarrels, fighting, hatred, and malice in their relationships must plant these fifteen seeds (characters) of true love in that relationship.

Anyone who wants to prevent divorce and enjoy a long lasting marriage must urgently start building that marriage on these essential pillars listed above. These are God's blue print (original plan) of truelove, the DNA of real love. Without them, you get imitation (human – love), which is the opposite of genuine love.

Love is Patient and Kind

Let's begin with Patience and Kindness. True love is patient and kind. For a marriage to last long, couples must learn to be patient with each other and kind to each other. When partners fail to express patience and kindness in a relationship, they are bound to have constant quarrels and fights that may eventually lead to divorce.

Who wants to stay with an impatient man! Who wants to stay with an impatient woman! One of the greatest killers of relationships and marriages is impatience. Conversely, one of the greatest pillars of long lasting marriages is patience. When couples are patient with each other, they accommodate each other's weakness and gives time to the other partner to improve, to grow, to become stronger and better. When couples are able to tolerate each other through their learning and growing process, they eventually become better individuals and enjoy a long-lasting marriage. If a man flares up at every little mistake his wife makes and begins to beat her, it's a sign that he lacks patience. If a woman begins to nag at every little fault of her husband, it shows that she lacks patience. Most quarrels in marriages are a result of lack of patience.

Without patience, marriages die. Without patience divorce is inevitable. If you want your marriage to last, you must be patient with your partner. If you ask long-married couples how they were able to keep a successful marriage, many of them would tell you that patience is the secret. They would tell you that they learnt to tolerate and accommodate each other's weaknesses. Unfortunately, most young couples lack the ability to tolerate their partners. They want to force the other person into a mold that they have imagined in their head. They want to hurriedly change the other person without understanding that change is a gradual process and takes time. Whenever you fail to tolerate and be patient with your partner, stress, strife, quarrel and fighting will set in and put a strain on your marriage. Instead of creating tension in your marriage, try and overlook little faults, speak the truth in love, do not flare up or raise your voice at your partner, be understanding and forebear some things as you both move towards becoming better individuals.

"Relationships be it dating or marriage, can be viewed as the needle and thread. You cannot sew a fabric with just the needle or the thread. You will need both to get started. It takes patience to thread the needle. The more you learn the technique, the better you will get at it in the future. The same applies to your relationship. Be patient with each other."
— Kemi Sogunle

Apart from patience, another key ingredient to a successful marriage is to build your marriage on kindness. There are no successful marriages that didn't have kindness as one of their building blocks. Kindness is the quality of being friendly, generous, and considerate. No marriage lasts which is void of friendship, generosity and fair consideration. The whole world recognizes kindness and responds positively to it.

Kindness is the language which the deaf can hear and the blind can see. -Mark Twain

Even among mere friends or strangers, kindness fosters unity and love, and ends rage, quarrels and malice, let alone within marriage. It changes everything for good. Kindness is a universal language. Everyone understands it. Marriages can last forever if couples are friendly and generous to each other.

In times of misunderstanding, show kindness to your partner. Even when you are offended by your partner or your partner is offended at you, show kindness. When there is tension in the home and your partner expects you to be angry, show kindness. Kindness has the power to soften the hardest heart and turn away rage. It does not matter how difficult you think your spouse is, when you show him or her kindness, they will respond positively.

Prideful and Boastful Love

Marriage has but one enemy—pride. It decays a marriage from the inside out.
-Kevin A. Thompson

True love is neither prideful nor boastful. When couples are boastful or proud in their attitude, they will find it difficult to lead a peaceful marriage. Prideful people do not admit their mistakes or say sorry for their wrongs. Any marriage where the partners are too proud to apologize to each other will sooner or later crash. Most marriages actually end in divorce because one or both partners are too proud to say sorry. Whenever couples cannot bury their ego and admit their wrongs, they put unnecessary stress on their relationship. Prolonged anger, malice, lack of forgiveness etc. exist in marriages because of pride. If we can bury our pride, we would have automatically buried malice, un-forgiveness, and perpetual anger.

If we can humble ourselves before our partners, we would enjoy a peaceful and happy marriage. Unfortunately, most men around the world define their manhood by how much pride and ego they have. Have you ever heard men say that it is ego that makes a man a real man? That is the number one problem in marriages: ego, pride, self-centeredness. When men want to become Lords over their wives and treat them as slaves, they eventually get into trouble that most times leads to divorce. Why? The reason is that true love can never thrive where there is pride. Anywhere you find pride, know that true love is lacking there. True love by nature is humble and meek. Jesus Christ our savior humbled himself by living heaven to earth to die for the church. We didn't deserve it but he did it for us. That is true love. He humbled himself and died a sinner's death. He took our place even though we didn't deserve him. That is how every man should humble himself before his wife. We must model Jesus in our marriages. If a man allows pride to rule his marriage, that same pride will ruin the marriage. Pride always precedes a fall. To keep your marriage standing, you must kick out the enemy called pride.

Although men are mostly blamed for expressing pride in marriage, some women are also very proud and boastful. If a woman is proud and boastful before her husband, she will ruin her marriage by herself. Pride whether expressed by husbands or wives has the capacity to destroy marriages faster than anything else could.

Most relationships fail because couples fight with pride more than they work with love.
-Anonymous

Let me share a story of a woman who destroyed her marriage because of pride with you. She wrote the following article:
"How I Ruined My Marriage Because Of Pride"

I am writing to you in order to make someone understand that it's good to appreciate our partners despite their flaws.

I am 32 years old. My ex hubby & I dated for six years. We were best of friends, I waited until he completed college and started work, my family and his family then met, we got married and had a son. (7 years old now).

My husband was short tempered at times, but our problems started when I wanted to make him feel he couldn't control me.

Every time we argued, I would pack my bags, go to my family and explain. My sisters would phone my husband and shout at him. If he was controlling me I would always dare him that if he wished, he could divorce me.

I never wanted divorce, I just had pride and I never wanted to look like a loose woman in his eyes. One day I pushed him so hard that for the first time he beat me and locked me outside. I went to my family; my family took him to the police, every time I looked like I was being abused! But to be honest, I used to abuse my husband emotionally. He was arrested and detained. I was asked by his family to withdraw the case, I felt that what I was doing was wrong.

My husband was never a violent man, he did what he did because I pushed him to the wall of which he openly knelt down and apologized. I withdrew the charge, and we reconciled. After three months, I packed my bags after a small issue, and he remained alone. After two days I received a call that he was in the hospital, my family told me that I shouldn't go there because it would look like I was begging him, and my sisters believed he was feigning the illness.

All this time, people felt sorry for me like I was the one being abused. He spent a week in the hospital, after he came out, I just received a divorce summon. I wanted to say no to divorce, but because I felt this pride, I wanted him to change his mind and beg me. I called him and said he would get the divorce because I lived like I was in hell.

When we went to court, I wanted to make him pay, so I told the court that I needed his properties to be shared. To my surprise he openly told the court that whatever he and I acquired together should be given to me, all he wanted was divorce. We were divorced in 2009 July.

Now, this Saturday (today) my husband is marrying, whilst I am here wasted! My family members are gossiping about me, I depend on what my ex gives to my son for survival. I know I wasted my marriage. I am here telling all wives that they should be careful how they get advice.

Don't be cheated, don't entertain family interference in your marriage my dear reader. Even my young sisters are much more respected than me. Those who encouraged me to get divorced are always teasing and bad mouthing me. Please ladies, be vigilant in your marriage. I thought it wise to share my story to save your marriage. There is no benefit in pride for nothing.[1]

From the story above, you could see that pride will always lead to disaster and destruction as the bible stated:

Pride goes before destruction, a haughty spirit before a fall

Proverb 16:18(NIV)

If you want a lasting marriage, do away with pride and humble yourself before your spouse. This becomes easy to achieve when couples have true love for each other.

Whenever couples express Agape love in their marriages, pride dies a natural death. It is not found in such a home. Humility in marriage fosters intimacy, friendship, forgiveness and peace.

Before I bring the chapter to a close I would like to list some warning signs of a prideful marriage or relationship.[2]

1. When everything revolves around you or is about you.
2. When you are always finding fault with your partner
3. When you refuse to be positively influenced by your spouse
4. When you ignore or can't even see the needs of your spouse
5. When you always seek attention.
6. When you refuse to seek wise counsel from people of authority (experts, counselors, parents,).
7. When your viewpoint is the only correct viewpoint.
8. When you feel too important to ask for help but always expect to be served.
9. When you cannot sacrifice anything or submit your will or goals for the sake of the marriage.

10.	When you refuse to say "I'm sorry."

Whenever you see any of these signs in your marriage, know that pride is ruling your marriage and if care is not taken, it will ruin it. These signs also show that Agape love is lacking in that marriage. Wherever Agape love is pride cannot be found there. True love is not boastful nor pride! True love is patient and kind!

Nuggets

1. The best thing a man can do for himself and his wife is to make sure that their marriage is built upon the DNA of true love. Couples must learn the traits of true love and make a conscious effort to imbibe them and live by them.

2. True love is built upon the foundation of 15 seeds or characteristics which when expressed have the capacity to keep marriages forever. Whoever builds their love on these seeds will have a long lasting marriage.

3. The foundations you build your marriage or relationships on determine the outcome. If you build on the foundation of truelove, you will have a marriage on the rock and it will never fail. But if you build your marriage on human love (lust), it will fail because you have built on a shallow foundation.

4. Anyone who wants to put an end to the quarrels, fighting, hatred, and malice in their relationships must plant the fifteen seeds (characters) of true love in that relationship. Anyone who wants to prevent divorce and enjoy a long lasting marriage must urgently start building that marriage on these essential pillars (traits) of true love.

5. For a marriage to last long, couples must learn to be patient with each other and kind to each other. When partners fail to express patience and kindness in a relationship, they are bound to have constant quarrels and fights that may eventually lead to divorce.

6. One of the greatest pillars of long lasting marriages is patience. When couples are patient with each other, they accommodate each other's weakness and gives time to the other partner to

improve, to grow, to become stronger and better. When couples are able to tolerate each other through their learning and growing process, they eventually become better individuals and enjoy a long-lasting marriage.

7. Most quarrels in marriages are a result of lack of patience. Without patience, marriages die. Without patience divorce is inevitable. If you want your marriage to last, you must be patient with your partner.

8. Whenever you fail to tolerate and be patient with your partner, stress, strife, quarrel and fighting will set in and put a strain on your marriage. Instead of creating tension in your marriage, try and overlook little faults, speak the truth in love, do not flare up or raise your voice at your partner, be understanding and

forebear some things as you both move towards becoming better individuals.

9. In times of misunderstanding, show kindness to your partner. Even when you are offended by your partner or your partner is offended at you, show kindness. When there is tension in the home and your partner expects you to be angry, show kindness. Kindness has the power to soften the hardest heart and turn away rage. It does not matter how difficult you think your spouse is, when you show him or her kindness, they will respond positively.

10. Most marriages actually end in divorce because one or both partners are too proud to say sorry. Whenever couples cannot bury their ego and admit their wrongs, they put unnecessary stress on their relationship. Prolonged anger, malice, lack of forgiveness etc. exist in marriages because of pride. If we can

bury our pride, we would have automatically buried malice, un-forgiveness, and perpetual anger. If we can humble ourselves before our partners, we would enjoy a peaceful and happy marriage.

11.   This is the number one problem in marriages: ego, pride, self-centeredness. When men want to become Lords over their wives and treat them as slaves, they eventually get into trouble that most times leads to divorce. Why? The reason is that true love can never thrive where there is pride. Anywhere you find pride, know that true love is lacking there. True love by nature is humble and meek.

12.   If a man allows pride to rule his marriage, that same pride will ruin the marriage. Pride always precedes a fall. To keep your marriage standing, you must kick out the enemy called pride.

Chapter Five

As Christ Loved the Church

Chapter Five
As Christ Loved the Church

One of the most important principles for a successful marriage and unfortunately the least understood of all marriage principles is to love your wife as Christ loved the church. Many men have a list of things they expect their wives to do if they want a lasting and peaceful marriage. They know so much about the dos and don'ts that their wives must obey but know little or nothing about loving their wives as Christ loved the church. When marriages fail, men are quick to put the blame on their wives and exonerate themselves. It is my opinion that instead of blaming women all the time for failed marriages, men should rather take responsibility and ask themselves some questions. The most important question I think every man should ask himself is "do I love my wife as Christ loved the church?" We shall be discussing that question in this chapter. I encourage you to pay keen attention to everything you are about to discover as it could turn your marriage around for good.

Do Men Love Like Christ?

The blueprint for a successful marriage has already been laid down in scriptures. God was kind enough to have provided the formula, the algorithm and principles of long-lasting relationships for all of humanity. He did not leave us in the dark to wander and search aimlessly for how we could make our marriages work. He did not leave us in oblivion regarding peaceful and successful marriage. He laid a foundation for us and documented the principles that keep marriages forever in the scriptures for us. Unfortunately, most marriages including that of Christian couples still fail because of ignorance of what true love is. There is a huge ignorance of the principles of successful and lasting marriages in our society today.

Men all over the world are looking for submissive women while women are looking for men who would truly love them. The paradox however is that men do not know how to love women as they should and hence women find it difficult to submit. If men can love their wives as Christ loves the church, I believe all marital issues would be solved and divorce would become a forgotten word. The blueprint to a successful marriage is for men to love their wives as Christ loved the church and gave himself for her.

25 Husbands, love your wives, just as Christ also loved the church and gave Himself for her, 26 that He might sanctify and cleanse her with the washing of water by the word, 27 that He might present her to Himself a glorious church, not having spot or wrinkle or any such thing, but that she should be holy and without blemish. 28 So husbands ought to love their own wives as their own bodies; he who loves his wife loves himself. 29 For no one ever hated his own flesh, but nourishes and cherishes it, just as the Lord does the church. {Ephesians 5:25-29}

From the verses above, we see the greatest secret to a lasting and peaceful marriage. It says, *"Husbands, love your wives, just as Christ also loved the church and gave Himself for her"*.

If half the men in the world understand this secret and live by it", the rate of divorce, domestic violence, marital wars etc. would drastically reduce. If all Christian men who read this passage of scriptures understand what they are reading and practice it, divorce would become an alien term in the body of Christ. Future generation of Christians would scarcely hear or know the meaning of the word "divorce". Sadly, a greater percentage of men in the world, the church inclusive are completely ignorant of what it means to love their wives as Christ loved the church. Although this passage of scriptures is read in most marriage and relationship conferences, the truth however, is that not much emphasis is placed on this principle of loving your wife as Christ loved the church.

Most pastors and church leaders often read that passage of scriptures to oppress women and tell them about the need for submission. It is funny how men read that passage of the bible and see only what women must do but not what men should do. That is a proof that most men lack true love and are biased and egocentric. The greatest secret to a lasting marriage stares them in the face but they ignore it. They rather focus on verses that massage their ego. When eventually their marriages end in divorce, they put the blame on the women and accuse them of lack of submission. Men hardly ask themselves if they loved their wives as Christ loved the church. They hardly even imagine that the reason for their divorce could be linked to their lack of Agape love as Christ demonstrated it. I hold it to be true that if men can love their wives as Christ loved the church, almost all marital problems and divorce would die a natural death.

So, what does it mean to love your wife as Christ loved the church? To answer that question, we must first examine how Christ relates with the church.

Humanity was doomed and bound in sin. We were associated with all sorts of immorality and evil. We did wrong at will and enjoyed every bit of it. We were dirty, unholy, weak, and unrighteous and doomed for hell. We deserved eternal death as our punishment. The soul that sins ought to die and we all were guilty of multitudes of sin. However, what did God do? He sent his son Jesus, the one to whom we would marry, to this earth. Our groom, our husband came to earth to meet filthy humans like you and me. When he came, he saw firsthand how unfit, unqualified and incompatible we were with him. He had the right to judge us and condemn us. He had the right to say he would not marry such depraved creatures as humans. He would have done no wrong had he sentenced us to death for our sins; we deserved death.

However, instead of condemning us to death, he chose to die in our place. Instead of proving to us how holy and righteous he was and how filthy and sinful we were, he chose rather to spill his blood to wash and cleanse us from all sins and filth. We deserved to be hung on the cross and face crucifixion, but he chose the nails and the cross by himself and took our place. If we must get married to him, then we must become as pure and holy as he is. If we must unite with him, we must be cleansed and emerge spotless and blameless. Knowing fully well that we are weak and lack the capacity to attain such purity, he decided to put his life on the line and shed his life's blood for us. For he alone has the capacity to cleanse us. Only his blood could purge and sanctify us to such a spotless purity. Therefore, while we were yet sinners, Christ died for us. While we were yet God's enemies, Jesus gave his life to save us and to make our union with him possible. What a love that gives instead of make demands! What a love that understands another's weakness and helplessness! What a love that condemns not but justifies! What a love that takes upon himself the punishment that others deserve! That love is Agape! Christ has demonstrated this love for the church. He has modeled it for all to see. God has therefore commanded husbands to have such kind of love for their wives. That was exactly what the scripture meant when it says, *"Husbands, love your wives, just as Christ also loved the church and gave Himself for her"*.

This, here is the greatest secret to a lasting marriage. When husbands love their wives as Christ loves the church, they would do everything and give everything that is required to make their union last. Jesus gave his life to make his union with the church eternal. What can husbands give to save their marriage!

When men love their wives as Christ loved the church, they would not judge or condemn them for their weaknesses, excesses, or faults. They would rather forgive them and teach them the truth in love.

When husbands love their wives as Christ loved the church, they would not give them the punishment they deserve or pay them back any wrong that they commit. Husbands would rather take the blame and bear the cross as Christ did for the church. That is why I can tell you convincingly that men who beat their wives do not know what true love is. Men who condemn and judge their wives do not know what true love is. Men who reprise wrongdoings to their wives are ignorant of what true love is. The same is true for men who demand blamelessness and perfection from their wives; they are void of true love. True love does not demand it supplies! True love does not condemn it purifies and justifies. Imagine a world in which men love their wives as Christ loved the church. Such a world would know everlasting peace and joy in marriages. Divorce would be a forgotten word in such a world. Unfortunately, instead of men to love their wives as Christ loved the church, they are focusing on their faults and demanding submission from them.

Submission versus Domination

As I stated earlier, most men read the scriptures and see only why women should submit to them but never see why they should love their wives unconditionally. This is particularly true for men of the 3rd world. Most 3rd world countries like Nigeria, Ghana, and the majority of African countries where Christianity or Islam is the prevailing religion, most men Lord it over women and demand submission from their wives forcefully. These men have not the slightest idea what true love really means. There are only few marriage seminars in Church where submission is not the subject of discussion. There is hardly a women's conference where the bulk of the discussion is not on how women should submit to their husbands. I must say here, that while submission in itself is not a bad thing, I however, believe that men ought not to demand submission from their wives but to love them unconditionally.

The reason I say this is that, wherever true love is, submission will automatically be found there. If men express Agape love for their wives, they would naturally submit to them. They would not need to demand for it. There is hardly a woman who has experienced true love from her husband who will not willingly submit to him.

In my opinion, women are generally submissive. The problem most times is not with wives but with husbands. Most husbands today have gone beyond seeking just submission to seeking worship. They want their wives to worship them and see them as Lord. They say that men are supposed to dominate. While that may be true, it is however a lie that, men are supposed to dominate over women (wives). The bible never taught that. Instead it teaches that man (male and female) should dominate not over each other but over the fish of the sea and the bird of the air and over all creeping creatures.

26 Then God said, "Let us make mankind in our image, in our likeness, so that they may rule over the fish in the sea and the birds in the sky, over the livestock and all the wild animals,[a] and over all the creatures that move along the ground." 27 So God created mankind in his own image, in the image of God he created them; male and female he created them. 28 God blessed them and said to them, "Be fruitful and increase in number; fill the earth and subdue it. Rule over the fish in the sea and the birds in the sky and over every living creature that moves on the ground."
Genesis 1:26-28(NIV)

From the verses above, we see that the charge to have dominion over the earth was given to both male and female. It is therefore an aberration for men to seek to dominate over their wives. God never intended it to be so from the beginning.

This desire in men to dominate over their wives is the reason for so many quarrels, fights and divorce in marriages. When men seek Lordship, worship or dominion, they subjugate and subject their wives to all sorts of ill treatments. Men often treat their wives as slaves just because they seek worship and Lordship. Instead of men to grow together with their wives in wisdom, might and understanding so as to both dominate over the earth, they rather oppress and suppress them. That desire to suppress a woman with whom you have become one in marriage is a proof of lack of true love. True love does not oppress, subject or subjugate another. True love reaches down to lift others up, let alone the one you have chosen to spend the rest of your life with. Men ought to serve their wives if they desire to be the head. Jesus said he who wants to become the head must first become a servant. Men who truly love their wives will serve them, build them, teach them and raise them up so that they both could rule over the earth and do exploits. In this process of growing together and ruling together husbands and wives submit themselves one to another as the need arises. Sometimes, women surrender their will to their husbands and at other times, men surrender their will to their wives. This is good as long as it is for the greater good of the family. True love thrives wherever both parties submit to each other.

21 Submit to one another out of reverence for Christ.

Ephesians 5:21(NIV)

So instead of men seeking to dominate over their wives and demanding submission from them, husbands and wives should submit to each other and express true love for each other. That is how to build a successful and long lasting marriage.

The Love That Purifies

Before I bring this chapter to a close, I would like to encourage you to practice the kind of love that seeks to rather purify and strengthen the other person instead of that which criticizes and condemns. Whether you like it or not, you will never find a perfect person on this side of eternity. Our planet is made up of people with weaknesses, flaws, dents, and shortcomings. You too are one of them. Hence, instead of seeking a perfect spouse and constantly criticizing your partner, remember that you too are not perfect and look for ways to make your partner a better person while your partner does the same to you. If we must criticize in marriages, let it be constructive criticism; the kind that seeks to make the other person better and not to humiliate or provoke.

The thing is that love gives us a ringside seat on somebody else's flaws, so of course you're gonna spot some things that kinda need to be mentioned. But often the romantic view is to say, 'If you loved me, you wouldn't criticize me.' Actually, true love is often about trying to teach someone how to be the best version of themselves.

-Alain de Botton

Our goal in relationship should be to help our partner become the best versions of who they were created to be. True love purifies and nourishes. From the verses we read earlier, we saw the secret of a long lasting marriage: *Husbands, love your wives, just as Christ also loved the church and gave Himself for her, that He might sanctify and cleanse her with the washing of water by the word, that He might present her to Himself a glorious church, not having spot or wrinkle or any such thing, but that she should be holy and without blemish.*

From the foregoing, we see that husbands have a responsibility to cleanse their wives and purify them. That means that women will always have one weakness or the other. They will always have one fault or another. It is the responsibility of every man to discover where his wife needs strengthening, cleansing, purification or enlightenment.

If your wife has a weakness in the area of cleanliness, teach her how to be clean in a loving and romantic manner. That is purification. If your wife has a fault in the area of cooking, teach her or enroll her in a catering school. That is purification. If her shortcoming is in the area of financial management, tutor her on how to wisely spend money. If she has challenges with spoken English, get her a private tutor. If she is not romantic, teach her to become romantic. Whatever it is that you notice is a fault or a lack in your wife, do not criticize her; fix it. That is purification. Keep upgrading and building her until she becomes the best of herself. Gold goes through several processes of purification before it becomes attractive and its value visible. Women have so much gifts, virtues, worth and potentials. A true man would purify and enable his wife to become the best she could be.

Marriage relationships will be full of joy, peace and last long if men know how to love their wives as Christ loved the church.

By way of summarizing this chapter, it is needful to remind you that the Biblical injunction in Ephesians 5:25 "Husbands, love your wives, just as Christ loved the church and gave himself up for her" is only possible when a man has the love of Christ in his heart. This is so because truelove is of the heart (the real you), hence the symbol of the heart. Regarding submission and respect, I will not fail to mention here that women with the knowledge of truelove always respect and submit to their husbands. It is worthy of note that the first need of a man is respect and that of a woman is True love. A lady once said to me "Is it only the wife that should respect the husband, what about the husband respecting the wife?" and I answered her "any man that has True love for his wife, makes her the queen, she comes first in his life after God, he opens the car door for her etc. his respect for the wife is automatic. Take a look at the fifteen characters of true love that the husbands are to give their wives, you will find that, they put their wives first before themselves, and the wives ought to do the same also, that is true love. A marriage that is built on true love will always last forever as the husband loves his wife unconditionally and the wife respects the husband in return.

Nuggets

1. Many men have a list of things they expect their wives to do if they want a lasting and peaceful marriage. They know so much about the dos and don'ts that their wives must obey but know little or nothing about loving their wives as Christ loved the church.

2. When marriages fail, men are quick to put the blame on their wives and exonerate themselves. It is my opinion that instead of blaming women all the time for failed marriages, men should rather take responsibility and ask themselves some questions. The most important question I think every man should ask himself is "do I love my wife as Christ loved the church?"

3. Men all over the world are looking for submissive women while women are

looking for men who would truly love them. The paradox however is that men do not know how to love women as they should and hence women find it difficult to submit.

4. If men can love their wives as Christ loves the church, I believe all marital issues would be solved and divorce would become a forgotten word. The blueprint to a successful marriage is for men to love their wives as Christ loved the church and gave himself for her.

5. ". If half the men in the world understand this secret of loving their wives as Christ loved the church and live by it", the rate of divorce, domestic violence, marital wars etc. would drastically reduce. If all Christian men will understand this secret and practice it, divorce would become an alien term in the body of Christ. Future generation of Christians would scarcely

hear or know the meaning of the word "divorce".

6. I hold it to be true that if men can love their wives as Christ loved the church, almost all marital problems and divorce would die a natural death.

7. When men love their wives as Christ loved the church, they would not judge or condemn them for their weaknesses, excesses, or faults. They would rather forgive them and teach them the truth in love.

8. When husbands love their wives as Christ loved the church, they would not give them the punishment they deserve or pay them back any wrong that they commit. Husbands would rather take the blame and bear the cross as Christ did for the church.

9. I can tell you convincingly that men who beat their wives do not know what true

love is. Men who condemn and judge their wives do not know what true love is. Men who reprise wrongdoings to their wives are ignorant of what true love is. The same is true for men who demand blamelessness and perfection from their wives; they are void of true love. True love does not demand it supplies! True love does not condemn it purifies and justifies.

10.   Imagine a world in which men love their wives as Christ loved the church. Such a world would know everlasting peace and joy in marriages. Divorce would be a forgotten word in such a world.

11.   Wherever true love is, submission will automatically be found there. If men express Agape love for their wives, they would naturally submit to them. They would not need to demand for it. There is

hardly a woman who has experienced true love from her husband who will not willingly submit to him.

12. In my opinion, women are generally submissive. The problem most times is not with wives but with husbands. Most husbands today have gone beyond seeking just submission to seeking worship. They want their wives to worship them and see them as Lord.

13. This desire in men to dominate over their wives is the reason for so many quarrels, fights and divorce in marriages. When men seek Lordship, worship or dominion, they subjugate and subject their wives to all sorts of ill treatments.

14. Men often treat their wives as slaves just because they seek worship and Lordship. Instead of men to grow together with their wives in wisdom, might and understanding so as to both

dominate over the earth, they rather oppress and suppress them.

15.	That desire to suppress a woman with whom you have become one in marriage is a proof of lack of true love. True love does not oppress, subject or subjugate another. True love reaches down to lift others up, let alone the one you have chosen to spend the rest of your life with.

Chapter Six

The Real Picture of Love

Chapter Six
The Real Picture of Love

I have been trying to explain the meaning of true love from the first chapter of this book and I believe you now have some level of understanding about the meaning and nature of true love. In this chapter, I shall describe the real picture of true love and expand on the characteristics of such love. I believe that when love is exhibited in its real form, it would keep marriages and relationships together. I understand that there are millions of married couples around the world who claim to love each other truly and yet exhibit traits that are contradictory to the very nature of true love. I therefore find it needful to do an exposition on the real picture of true love to further enlighten you on the real meaning of true love.

Love Is Not Rude

The word 'rude' means to be offensively impolite or bad-mannered. True love is not rude. If you truly love someone, you will not be rude to him or her. If you intentionally offend someone, you cannot claim to love that person. When couples are rude to each other, it is a proof that they lack true love for each other.

Couples, who love their partners, would not belittle their partners in public. Wherever there is true love, there is no room for rudeness. Husbands and wives with true love for each other have great respect for each other. You must understand that you are one with your spouse. Whenever you are rude to your wife/husband, you are rude to yourself.

Love Is Not Self – Seeking

To me love is passionate, it is honest, and it is selfless. Love is willing to completely give up your life for someone, to make sacrifices and put them first.

-Benjamin Stone

In addition to love being patient and kind, humble and not boastful as was discussed in chapter four, you need to know also that love is not self-seeking. This means that love is not selfish or egocentric. True love is the other person-focused not self-centered. While this ought to be the obtainable norm in most families, it is however painful to state here that most marriages today are built on pure egocentrism and selfishness.

Do not take my word for it. The statistics of failed marriages, domestic violence, single motherhood, abandoned children and the many other relationship problems that plague our societies are a proof that majority of people in relationships and marriages are egocentric. If we take a critical look at the reason for all of the above mentioned relationship crisis, we would find that selfishness, and egocentrism and self-centeredness are at the very root of it. No one wants to lay down his will for another. Everyone wants his or her opinion to be superior and his or her decisions to be final. Everyone wants his or her needs to be met first before that of their spouse. When couples quarrel over little issues and divorce at the slightest provocation are they not self-seeking!

When men refuse to eat the available food and force their pregnant wives to cook whatsoever meal they crave, is that not self-centeredness! When men are only concerned about their wives satisfying them sexually and care not about the emotional and sexual needs of their wives, are they not being selfish!

True love on the other hand is others-focused; it always considers the other partner first. One of the ways to test and ascertain if a supposed love is real or not is to check if that love values or thinks of the other person before thinking of self. Any love that puts others first is true. Any love that shows "self-first" is a fake love.

For me, love is magic; it's about trust and understanding. It's putting the other person before you effortlessly. -A. R. Hydari

If your love is selfless it would forgive others no matter what they have done to you. When couples retaliate when offended instead of forgive their partners, it shows that they lack true love.

If your love is selfless it would bear the burden, pain and troubles of others instead of being indifferent. If couples cannot give a helping hand, a smile, moral support, care, financial assistance etc. to their partner in their time of pain and crisis, then true love is lacking in that relationship.

I must say here that while we all need to exhibit selfless love for others and our spouse inclusive, no one can truly demonstrate selfless love until he has known God. Selfless love is the nature of God and those who do not know him will have a hard time understanding why they should consider others before themselves or care for others before themselves. Human love is always selfish and couples who run their homes based on human love always suffer marital crisis that often leads to divorce. The only way to truly and perpetually live a selfless life is to know God and emulate Him.

Only God can give us a selfless love for others, as the Holy Spirit changes us from within. This is one reason we must receive Christ, for apart from His Spirit we can never be freed from the chains of selfishness, jealousy, and indifference. Will others see Christ's love in your life today?

Billy Graham

While it is true that people who do not know God will often have a hard time understanding selfless love, it is however also a fact that most Christian couples who claim to know God still exhibit selfishness and egocentrism in their marriages. This happens because they have not taken time to consciously walk with the Holy Spirit and allow him teach them the nature of true love.

Most Christian couples are often too busy to study the word of God and learn the nature of true love as demonstrated in the scriptures. The word of God has the answer to the problem of selfishness, egocentrism and pride that is destroying most marriages Christians' inclusive. Yet not many couples give themselves to the study of the word and build their home after it. One of such answers to the problem of selfishness is in the biblical injunction below:

Do nothing out of selfish ambition or vain conceit. Rather, in humility value others above yourselves

Philippians 2:3 (NIV)

From the verses above, we see the apostle Paul admonishing us to get rid of selfishness and in humility value others above ourselves. Oh! How peaceful and sweet marriages would be if every couple would imbibe this instruction and live by it! Imagine a home in which the man values his wife above himself and the woman values her husband above herself. Imagine a home in which wives care for their husbands first and husbands care for their wives first. Such a home would be heaven on earth. It does not matter how many marriage counselors we visit or how many marriage magazines we read, if we cannot humble ourselves and get rid of selfishness, our marriages will never know peace and true joy.

If couples must enjoy peace and harmony in their homes, they must demonstrate the true selfless love of God for each other. The kind of love that seeks the welfare of the other person above personal satisfaction is the only possible way to a joyful and peaceful marriage.

There is one and only one possible road to joy: selfless love.

Peter Kreeft

Love Is Not Easily Angered

One of the greatest enemies to a successful and long lasting marriage is anger. When women fall in love, they envisage a beautiful marriage, a peaceful home full of joy and expressions of love. Unfortunately, most women discover only after marriage that the man who has demonstrated so much self-control and affection during courtship is a shadow of himself. They find out that their supposed harmless husband has suddenly turned into an angry monster and a wife-beater.

It is a common thing for men with only natural love or Eros love to pretend during courtship and make women fall in love with them thinking that they are harmless and gentle. They show their true color only after they have successfully tied the knot and have their wives living with them under the same roof.

Have you ever heard of men beating their wives or stabbing their partners with a knife? Have you seen men drag their wives on the hair along the road during a fight? Have you seen husbands who strip their wives naked in public because of a quarrel that led to a fight? The statistics of women and men facing domestic violence in marriages across the world is alarming.

On average, 24 people per minute are victims of rape, physical violence or stalking by an intimate partner in the United States — more than 12 million women and men over the course of a year.

Nearly, 15% of women (14.8%) and 4% of men have been injured as a result of IPV(Intimate Partner Violence) that included rape, physical violence and/or stalking by an intimate partner in their lifetime.

1in 4 women (24.3%) and 1 in 7 men (13.8%) aged 18 and older in the United States have been the victim of severe physical violence by an intimate partner in their lifetime.

IPV alone affects more than 12 million people each year.[1]

Why is there so much intimate partner violence in a world that talks a lot about a love? The answer is simple; most of the people in the world do not know what true love is. Human love, Eros love is prevalent in the world and it lacks the ability to control one's emotions. Anger and intimate partner violence thrives only where Agape love is lacking. It is therefore not a surprise to me that we have such a terrible statistics of domestic violence.

Not too long ago, a married woman, Ronke Shonde who was in her mid-thirties was allegedly beaten to death by her husband, at their home. The alleged wife Killer was said to have killed his 37 years old wife, Ronke, by giving her fist blow which led to her death, on May 5, at the residence in Egbeda, Lagos.[2]

According to reports, the depot worker had beaten his wife to death around 8:30pm on Friday, May 5, 2016, at their place of residence. The couple had lived with their two kids at Tiemo Close in Egbeda area of Lagos state.[3]

Another man killed his wife in Delhi after he suspected her of having an affair. The accused first stabbed his wife to death and later chopped her body into pieces. He then dumped his wife's body, which he chopped into pieces, in a septic tank near their house. After the act, the accused visited the nearby police station to confess his crime.[4]

What do you think is responsible for all these domestic violence and murder? The answer is anger, excessive anger. When men can't control their emotions, they get inflamed or infuriated to the extent that they beat and in some cases murder their wives. True love is not easily angered. Such love that permits wife-beating and murder and say that it doesn't matter is not of God. It is human, Eros and fake. Agape love does not murder, beat a partner or scold another. It speaks truth in love not out of anger. Most marriages have been destroyed by anger and inability to control one's emotions. Until we learn Agape love, we cannot lead peaceful marriages. Until we are grounded in the love of God, anger and domestic violence will continually destroy our marriages. The answer therefore, is to learn the true love of God, Agape and allow it rule our marriages and home. True love is not easily angered and is non-violent.

Love Keeps No Records of Wrongs

One of the greatest demonstrations of God's love for humanity as recorded in the bible is found in Psalms of David:

3 If you, Lord, kept a record of sins, Lord, who could stand? 4 But with you there is forgiveness, so that we can, with reverence, serve you

Psalms 130:3-4

From the scriptures above, we see what it means to truly love another. One of the greatest demonstrations or proof of love in my opinion is to never keep record of wrongs but instead forgive the wrongdoer.

The heart which has learnt to forgive and let go of offence has truly known love. Most marital problems that eventually lead to divorce are a result of one partner keeping record of the wrongs of the other partner. Partners keep malice with each other for a long time because of the human desire to keep record of wrongs and possibly reprise the same. True love does not keep record of wrongs. True love forgives and restores. It covers a multitude of sins.

When couples cannot forgive each other and keep reminding each other of their sins or mistakes, then it is clear that they lack Agape love. True love says" your sins and iniquities I will remember no more!" Can you imagine how sweet marriage would be if partners learn to forgive each other of their wrongs and not keep a record of it! It would be heaven on earth.

Other Characteristics of Love

We have been mentioning different characteristics of true love that make marriages and relationships peaceful and long-lasting. These characteristics hold the solution to all the marital problems that plague couples all around the world. As we have already mentioned, love is not self – seeking, not easily angered, and does not keep records of wrongs. In addition to these and other characteristics mentioned in the previous chapter are "love does not rejoice in evil but rejoices in the truth". This means that love would always desire what is right and hate what is evil. If we have true love for others, we would not rejoice when evil befalls them or even think of hurting them. True love will think only about how to do well to others and not about doing wrong to them. When both partners rejoice in truth and abhor evil, then they will both enjoy a peaceful marriage.

 I would like to urge you and couples all over the world who want their marriages to last to endeavor to imbibe these characteristics of love into your lives and homes if you want a long lasting relationship.

Furthermore, love perseveres; that means that it bears all things. True love is easy and does not cost you. But you must make a choice to have true love and believe in it. I made the choice to believe in true love and that singular choice gave me so much peace in my marriage. I did everything I could to have a peaceful marriage. That includes perseverance. If the wife plays her role, she also will have peace in her marriage. Anyone that refuses to play his or her roles always pays a heavy price. All I do is to have a good understanding of my own part in the marriage, which is giving her true love. My role is to shower her with true love.

I love her through her faults and weaknesses. I bear, persevere, and accommodate her excesses. Yes! That is what true love means. Most men instead of give their wives true love, they try to change them. Man, you cannot change your wife, so concentrate on giving her True love and allow God to change her. The same is true for the wife.

Most problems in marriages are husbands and wives trying to change each other; and when they cannot do it, they develop anxiety, all kind of illnesses and diseases due to bitterness and lack of forgiveness. When you learn to bear all things, you will no longer be self-centered. Remember this: the worse sin in marriage is selfishness.

Nuggets

1. True love is the other person-focused not self-centered. While this ought to be the obtainable norm in most families, it is however painful to state here that most marriages today are built on pure egocentrism and selfishness.

2. The statistics of failed marriages, domestic violence, single motherhood, abandoned children and the many other relationship problems that plague our societies are a proof that majority of people in relationships and marriages are egocentric.

3. If we take a critical look at the reason for most of the relationship crisis in our society, we would find that selfishness; egocentrism and self-centeredness are at the very root of it.

4. True love is others-focused; it always considers the other partner first. Any love that puts others first is true. Any love that shows "self-first" is a fake love.

5. Human love is always selfish and couples who run their homes based on human love always suffer marital crisis that often leads to divorce. The only way to truly and perpetually live a selfless life is to know God and emulate Him.

6. It does not matter how many marriage counselors we visit or how many marriage magazines we read, if we cannot humble ourselves and get rid of selfishness, our marriages will never know peace and true joy.

7. If couples must enjoy peace and harmony in their homes, they must demonstrate the true selfless love of God for each other. The kind of love that seeks the welfare of the other person above

personal satisfaction is the only possible way to a joyful and peaceful marriage.

8. Agape love does not murder, beat a partner or scold another. It speaks truth in love not out of anger.

9. Until we learn Agape love, we cannot lead peaceful marriages. Until we are grounded in the love of God, anger and domestic violence will continually destroy our marriages. The answer therefore, is to learn the true love of God, Agape and allow it rule our marriages and home. True love is not easily angered and it's non-violent.

10.   One of the greatest demonstrations or proof of love in my opinion is to never keep record of wrongs but instead forgive the wrongdoer. The heart which has learnt to forgive and let go of offence has truly known love.

11.   True love does not keep record of wrongs. True love forgives and restores.

It covers a multitude of sins. When couples cannot forgive each other and keep reminding each other of their sins or mistakes, then it is clear that they lack Agape love. True love says" your sins and iniquities I will remember no more!"

Chapter Seven

Why Marriages Fail

Chapter Seven
Why Marriages Fail

The rate at which marriages fail nowadays is alarming and nobody is asking why. We can pretend as much as we want that it does not matter or that it does not bother us the drastic increase of divorce rate in our world, but whether we like it or not this is negatively affecting crime rate, abortion rate, illiteracy, poverty and many other vices in our society. Children that grow up from broken homes most likely suffer or become culprits of one or more social vices. It is therefore important that we discuss the reason for divorce and how to prevent it in our marriages. That is why we are going to discuss why marriages fail in this chapter.

I Never Thought We Would Have a Divorce

You don't sign up for a divorce when you get married. It's very painful. But it's taught me a great deal about myself.

-Dwayne Johnson

Marriage and divorce are both common experiences. In Western cultures, more than 90 percent of people marry by age 50. Healthy marriages are good for couples' mental and physical health. They are also good for children; growing up in a happy home protects children from mental, physical, educational and social problems. However, about 40 to 50 percent of married couples in the United States divorce. The divorce rate for subsequent marriages is even higher.[1]

All over the world, couples have divorce for one reason or the other. The number of children from broken homes is increasing proportionately. What could be responsible for this anomaly! Why are people walking away from the same marriage that they once dreamt of having. Why are spouses turning their backs on the partners they once desired recklessly? During marriage or wedding ceremonies, couples exchange vows to love each other forever and stay by each other forever; why do they forget those vows so easily and damn the consequences of breaking them? It is true that most people who get married expect their marriages to last forever. They exchange vows on the wedding day with the hope that those vows would hold true and keep the marriage forever.

However, many of them realize early that a happy and successful marriage is beyond the vows exchanged on the wedding day. It is beyond merely reciting a vow, it is a life of love to be demonstrated daily. If you ask most divorced couple if they envisaged a divorce prior to their marriage, the answer would be no. In fact you would most likely here words like "I never thought we would have a divorce". So, if most couples who divorced never thought they would have a divorce, why then is there many divorcees in our society?

It is especially unlikely in a world that talks so much about love to have people walk in and out of love as easily as is the case in modern times.

This suggests to me that most people who get married have not the slightest idea of what true love is. People easily break their marriage vows and walk away from their partners because they lack or do not understand the eternal and sacrificial nature of true love. I honestly think that the world needs more enlightenment and education on what true love really means. Teenagers, young adults and married couples need a reorientation on love and marriage. The world is bound to encounter a higher divorce rate and a proportionate increase in social vices if there is no urgent campaign to teach people about true love and how to build long-lasting marriages.

With the exception of a few cases of life-threatening domestic violence, most divorce cases are due to lack of understanding of the 15seeds or characteristics of true love. If people express a love that is patient and kind, they would hardly divorce their spouses. If couples have a love that is not envious or boastful, there will be a very low propensity for divorce. If partners demonstrate the kind of love that is humble and not self-seeking, divorce would be a difficult occurrence to come by. If couples relate with each other with a love that is not easily angered, divorce would naturally become extinct. If we all practice the true Agape love that keeps no record of wrongs, there would be no occasion for divorce.

So, it is obvious that divorce is prevalent in our world today because there is a gross ignorance of what true love means. "I never thought we would have a divorce" is the slogan of most divorcees today because they never had or understood true love; they only thought they had true love but it was human erotic love all along. No matter how often we talk about love or teach others about it, if we do not have true Agape love for our spouses it would eventually show and the result would be divorce.

Dad could talk about peace and love out loud to the world, but he could never show it to the people who supposedly meant the most to him: his wife and son. How can you talk about peace and love and have a family in bits and pieces - no communication, adultery, divorce? You can't do it, not if you're being true and honest with yourself.

-Julian Lennon

How I Ruined My Own Marriage

One reason people divorce amongst others is lack of attention and affection. Most men especially preachers are often so busy with ministry that they forget to create time for their spouse. A woman who truly loves her husband craves his attention and affection. When she doesn't get any of that, she begins to feel unwanted and unloved. This feeling soon turns into anger and frustration. A frustrated woman would naturally be easily angered and provoke arguments in the home. Men often do not understand this part of their wives and wonder why women easily get irritated. Men fail to realize that in as much as they are working hard to earn a living to take care of the family; they must never do that at the expense of their affection and attention for their wives.

The greatest gift you can give another is the purity of your attention.

Richard Moss

Whether you are a pastor, a doctor, an engineer or whatever your profession is, you must never put your profession above your marriage relationship and use that as an excuse to not give your wife the affection and attention she deserves. Women hate to be lonely in marriage. They feel abandoned by their husbands when he is too busy to spend time with them. So many marriages have fallen apart simply because of men's negligence. Marriages do not just break up, people break them. Successful and long-lasting marriage takes work. If your marriage is going to last, you must resolve to do everything possible to keep it. Otherwise, the end result would be divorce. If you do not pay attention to your wife, you would ruin your marriage unintentionally and will regret it in the end.

Let me share a story of a preacher who admitted to ruining his own marriage by being insensitive to his wife's need of affection and attention while travelling the world doing ministry. He is Bishop Noel Jones. This is what he had to say about his divorce: I believe that for whatever reason you divorced, you have to repent and I have had to repent. I do not know if that is one of the things that is at the back of my mind and subconsciously keeping me from taking a step forward or because of what I was taught. However, at the end of the day, I made a vow. I made a vow for better or for worse. And when you consider you making a vow for better or for worse, who defines what worse is? Since I have been divorced and I have dealt with people in various situations of their own lives, I have found that what I decided to divorce about or what broke us up was miniscule compared to what other people went through.

And if I were to give you an anecdote and one of my problems is that I really ruined my marriage in the name of God. If you want a lesson, I will give you a lesson. I am very ebullient and very intense about what I do. This is because I believe that you can't be as good as you ought to be and can't be the best that you should be if you are not very intense about this job. There is no question in my mind that I am very intense. I was totally ought of balance and I still am as it relates to preaching. And I ruined my marriage in the name of God because she was often times upset. We argued every time I had to leave. I was the last person who was picked up at the airport when I got back. When I got off the plane, they were closing the airport by the time she came to get me; I was standing with my bags. I was completely indignant because I felt that she was driving a 300/500 LCL. And who wants to get off the airplane and not have somebody to greet them. But what I failed to understand was that she didn't want me to go in the first place. So why should she hurry up to pick me up! We were arguing all the time I had to leave; I mean I was so out of balance: church on Sunday, bible class on Monday. I was gone until Saturday and sometimes until Sunday morning. What I failed to understand as a novice is that there is a very thing line or a very difficult distinction between the signatures of frustration and anger. Often times, anger is simply frustration. And I said "what do you want, I was a preacher when you met me. So how in the world when the doors are opening you would not allow me to go?" And we had to have this vicious debate when I am going to do what God has called me to do. What I failed to understand was that she did not marry a profession, she married a person. And so now my word to anybody who wants to take from this lesson is that each preacher must understand the significance of ministering to his own wife.

A pastor's wife should never ever feel like she's got to compete with the church or the ministry for her husband's affection and attention.[2]

From the foregoing, we see how insensitivity to a woman's needs ruin a marriage. Men must understand the greatest needs of their wives and supply it and women must understand the greatest needs of their husbands and supply it. That is how marriages work. Each person must satisfy the other person and put the other person before himself or herself. We must never become self-seeking but other-person focused. If we do this, then we would build successful and long lasting marriages.

True love is selfless. It is prepared to sacrifice. -Sadhu Vaswani

If The Unbelieving Depart!

Although there are many justifiable reasons for divorce today, God however does not like divorce. All through the scriptures, God explicitly made plain how he hates divorce and wants our marriages to last and be successful. Once, Jesus was asked a question about divorce by the Jews; if it was right for a man to put away his wife. Jesus gave a very stunning answer which in my opinion is God's intention for humanity.

When Jesus had finished saying these things, he left Galilee and went into the region of Judea to the other side of the Jordan. 2 Large crowds followed him, and he healed them there. 3 Some Pharisees came to him to test him. They asked, "Is it lawful for a man to divorce his wife for any and every reason?"4 "Haven't you read," he replied, "that at the beginning the Creator 'made them male and female,'

5 and said, 'For this reason a man will leave his father and mother and be united to his wife, and the two will become one flesh'? 6 So they are no longer two, but one flesh. Therefore what God has joined together, let no one separate."

(Matthew 19:1-6 NIV)

From the verses above, we see a very important question *"Is it lawful for a man to divorce his wife for any and every reason?"* This question is so significant because it describes the very state of our world today; a world in which people divorce for any and every reason. We live in a world in which people divorce at will and do not care about any body's opinion or what God thinks about divorce. This happens even among Christian couples who say they understand the ways of God and know him. Most of the divorce cases in our societies today are because of any and every reason.

Be that is it may, I am rather more interested in the answer that Jesus gave to the question. Jesus said that in the beginning God created male and female for a reason; so that they will unite with each other and become one flesh. That exactly is the desire of God for humanity; that a man and a woman should become one in unity. God wants union, reconciliation and togetherness not division and separation. That is why God does not like it when men divorce their wives and vice-versa. Divorce is against the original order of things as God created them for our lives.

Somebody may say "well the law in our society permits divorce". That was exactly the same thing the Pharisees asked Jesus:

7 "Why then," they asked, "did Moses command that a man give his wife a certificate of divorce and send her away?" 8 Jesus replied, "Moses permitted you to divorce your wives because your hearts were hard. But it was not this way from the beginning. 9 I tell you that anyone who divorces his wife, except for sexual immorality, and marries another woman commits adultery."10 The disciples said to him, "If this is the situation between a husband and wife, it is better not to marry. (Matthew 19:7-10 NIV)

Jesus' answer yet again is mind blowing. He said that Moses permitted divorce because of the hardness of heart of the people not because it was right to divorce a woman. Jesus further stated that from the beginning it was not so; i.e. divorce was not God's idea for humanity from the outset. In trying to make the Jews understand how evil it is to put away one's wife, Jesus told them that the only condition under which a man could divorce his wife is if she is guilty of sexual immorality. This is not to say that every man must put away their wives because of sexual immorality. We have already stated that love covers a multitude of sins and does not keep record of wrongs. True love would forgive a partner who is guilty of sexual immorality and still love through the faults. We have also before stated that Christ has not divorced and will not divorce his church, his bride for any reason and that men have been commanded to love their wives as Christ loved the church and gave himself for it. I know that this is a hard meat to bite to say that it is ok and Agape to forgive a partner who cheated on his/her spouse. Yes! True love is extraordinary and often unfathomable. The fact that true love forgives does not mean that a partner who cheated should continue to cheat and take pride in it. No! That will not be right and Godly. Husbands and wives with truelove do not intentionally cheat on each other. They know that they are one, and most of all they believe that their wives and husbands are the most handsome men and the most beautiful women to them. They therefore find it difficult to cheat on their wives or husbands. They don't deny that there are more beautiful women, more handsome men out there, but they have made their choices. So, their marriage becomes marriage made in heaven on earth, because it is built on the foundation of truelove.

It is wrong to commit sexual immorality. It is wrong to be unfaithful to your wife. That is why the Old Testament stated explicitly the punishment for unfaithfulness in marriage. Yes! The punishments for marital unfaithfulness are so severe in the Bible. You may say I don't believe the Bible; it doesn't stop you from facing the consequences.

Let us start with the men: *You cry out, "Why doesn't the Lord accept my worship?" I' will tell you why! Because the Lord witnessed the vows you and your wife when you were young. But you have been unfaithful to her, though she remained your faithful partner, the wife of your marriage vows".* (*Malachi 2: 14 NLT*)

Did you see that the man's unfaithfulness to his wife caused his prayers to be unaccepted? There is also punishment for the wife who is unfaithful to her marriage covenant: *"Surely her house leads down to death and her paths to the spirits of the dead. (Proverbs 2: 18 NIV) The man who visits her is doomed. He will never reach the paths of life".* (*Proverbs 2:19 NLT*)

These verses tell us that God frowns at unfaithfulness in marriage and we must never take advantage of the forgiveness that is in Christ to indulge in sexual immorality. A man who refuses to divorce his wife even though she is guilty of sexual immorality demonstrates true love but the woman who takes advantage of that forgiveness to perpetually indulge in adultery does not know love or have true love.

The same is the case with a man who is guilty of adultery. Whoever is forgiven much should love much. In other words, when we forgive our spouses faults and refuse to divorce them; that should build true love in them and prevent them from perpetually misbehaving. Wherever true love is, forgiveness is there and divorce will be lacking.

In trying to emphasize the desire of God for our marriages, Apostle Paul alluded to the fact which we already stated that God hates divorce and wants us to stay with our partners forever.

10 To the married I give this command (not I, but the Lord): A wife must not separate from her husband. 11 But if she does, she must remain unmarried or else be reconciled to her husband. And a husband must not divorce his wife. (1 Corinthians 7:10-11 NIV)

Here, we see that God has commanded us to never divorce our spouses. If we would adhere to the commands of God, we would enjoy peaceful, joyful and long-lasting marriages. One of the reasons for the huge failure rate of marriages is refusal to adhere to the principles of God for successful marriages. If we would love as Christ loves and follow his footstep, we would not have as much divorce rate in our society as we have today.

To further buttress his point about the desire of God for lasting unions, Paul the apostle said:

12 To the rest I say this (I, not the Lord): If any brother has a wife who is not a believer and she is willing to live with him, he must not divorce her. 13 And if a woman has a husband who is not a believer and he is willing to live with her, she must not divorce him. 14 For the unbelieving husband has been sanctified through his wife, and the unbelieving wife has been sanctified through her believing husband. Otherwise your children would be unclean, but as it is, they are holy. 15 But if the unbeliever leaves, let it be so. The brother or the sister is not bound in such circumstances; God has called us to live in peace. 16 How do you know, wife, whether you will save your husband? Or, how do you know, husband, whether you will save your wife? (1 Corinthians 7:12-16 NIV)

From these verses, we see that the apostle even went further to state that a believing man who is married to an unbelieving wife should not divorce her and vice-versa. He said that as long as the other partner is willing to stay in the marriage, there should be no divorce. What a piece of advice! I believe that the apostle was speaking the mind of God; as long as any man would come to Jesus, he will in no wise cast out. That means that anyone who is willing to be married to Christ will never be divorced. That is how couples should treat each other; as long as the weak partner is still pleased to remain with you, do not divorce him/her. Love her through her fault, love him through his faults. The only condition, under which a marriage should separate, is if the weak or guilty partner chooses to walk away. I however know that true love will chase after the object of its love.

True love - that is, deep, abiding love that is impervious to emotional whims or fancy - is a choice. It's a constant commitment to a person regardless of the present circumstances. --
Mark Manson

Nuggets

1. We must realize that a happy and successful marriage is beyond the vows exchanged on the wedding day. It is beyond merely reciting a vow, it is a life of love to be demonstrated daily.

2. People easily break their marriage vows and walk away from their partners because they lack or do not understand the eternal and sacrificial nature of true love.

3. The world is bound to encounter a higher divorce rate and a proportionate increase in social vices if there is no urgent campaign to teach people about true love and how to build long-lasting marriages.

4. If people express a love that is patient and kind, they would hardly divorce their spouses. If couples have a love that is not envious or boastful, there will be a very low propensity for divorce. If partners demonstrate the kind of love

that is humble and not self-seeking, divorce would be a difficult occurrence to come by. If couples relate with each other with a love that is not easily angered, divorce would naturally become extinct. If we all practice the true Agape love that keeps no record of wrongs, there would be no occasion for divorce.

5. No matter how often we talk about love or teach others about it, if we do not have true Agape love for our spouses it would eventually show and the result would be divorce.

6. A woman who truly loves her husband craves his attention and affection. When she doesn't get any of that, she begins to feel unwanted and unloved. This feeling soon turns into anger and frustration.

7. Men fail to realize that in as much as they are working hard to earn a living to take care of the family; they must never do

that at the expense of their affection and attention for their wives.

8. Women hate to be lonely in marriage. They feel abandoned by their husbands when he is too busy to spend time with them.

9. Marriages do not just break up, people break them. Successful and long-lasting marriage takes work. If your marriage is going to last, you must resolve to do everything possible to keep it. Otherwise, the end result would be divorce. If you do not pay attention to your wife, you would ruin your marriage unintentionally and will regret it in the end.

10. Men must understand the greatest needs of their wives and supply it and women must understand the greatest needs of their husbands and supply it. That is how marriages work. Each person must satisfy the other person and put the

other person before himself or herself. We must never become self-seeking but other-person focused. If we do this, then we would build successful and long lasting marriages.

Chapter Eight

The Struggle for Supremacy

Chapter Eight
The Struggle for Supremacy

A look at the life of the average couple in our society will reveal that there is a struggle between husbands and wives for supremacy. Husbands are trying to subjugate their wives and wives are trying hard to be free from slavery. In this chapter, we shall discuss why most couples have a slave-master relationship instead of a friendly husband-wife relationship.

The Slave-Master Relationship

It is an evidence of lack of true love for a man to treat or relate with his wife as a slave. This is particularly pronounced in Africa and in the middles east. Most African men were brought up with the mentality of superiority. They were raised in homes in which they constantly saw their father maltreating their mother and treating her like a slave.

In her book *I am A Woman I am A Human,* an African woman by the name Topsy Gift shared a story of how the slave-master relationship between her dad and mum almost prevented her from getting married because she thought that all men were the same. In her words she said:

"One of my fears, before I got married, was getting married to a man who would end up being like my biological father. I dreaded the thought of getting married to a man who would abuse me like my dad did my mum. At a point, I concluded that if every man was as my father, then I would rather remain unmarried than spend the rest of my life being a slave to a fellow human with a male superiority complex. Much of what I saw in my home while growing up was a slave-master-slave relationship with my dad being the slave master and my mum the slave"[1] (Excerpt from *I Am a Woman, I Am a Human* **by Topsy Gift**)

It breaks my heart to see several million women being treated as worthless objects and subjected to all kinds of abuse from the men who should love and protect them.
-Topsy Gift

The truth is that most men have been badly raised to believe that they are superior to women. A husband, who thinks that he is superior to his wife and that his decisions are supreme and must be accepted by his wife, is simply displaying his ignorance of what true love is and what it means to be united with his wife. Husband and wife should not be in a struggle for supremacy but rather should see each other as partners. The Bible records that a husband and his wife are not two different persons but one flesh. The day you got married to your partner, you became one with him or her. If two have become one flesh, why should there be a struggle for supremacy. To claim superiority over your wife is to claim superiority over yourself because you and your wife are one.

Peter alluded to this fact in his writings when he said:

7 Likewise, ye husbands, dwell with them according to knowledge, giving honor unto the wife, as unto the weaker vessel, and as being heirs together of the grace of life; that your prayers be not hindered. (1Peter 3:7 NIV)

In this verse, Apostle Peter encouraged husbands to respect and honor their wives because they are coheirs of the grace of life. This means that a woman is not a slave to her husband but a coheir or joint heir with him. You and your wife are partners not boss and slave. If you fail to honor your wife as a partner, your prayers will be hindered. Marriages in which men relate with their wives as partners last longer and are more peaceful and joyful than those in which the man is in a struggle for supremacy and treats his wife like a slave.

A Look at Eden

To find God's original idea for male-female relationships, we need to go to the very beginning before the fall of humanity. When God created humans, he did not create one gender superior and another gender inferior. Adam and his wife Eve were created equal. Although Adam was created before his wife Eve; that does not in any way suggest superiority or inferiority as many men claim. If the order of creation determines superiority, then we may conclude that the birds of the air and the fish of the sea are superior to humans since they were all created before humans. That of course will be a wrong ideology because we know that humans are of superior intelligence and nature to all other animals. Men therefore, should stop claiming superiority over their wives because they were created first.

Furthermore, it is important to note that men and women are created in the image of God. It is impossible for the image of God in a man to be superior to the image of God in a woman.

27 So God created mankind in his own image, in the image of God he created them; male and female he created them.

Genesis 1:27 (NIV)

If we want peaceful and joyful marriages, we must abandon the idea of supremacy and rather relate with each other as partners, coheirs and companions. Adam and his wife were created equal and they lived as partners before the fall of humanity. After the death and resurrection of Jesus Christ, the original order of things before the fall has been restored; no superiority, only equality.

Neither Male nor Female

In order to explain how we should relate with each other after the death and resurrection of Jesus Christ, Paul the apostle talked about the new creation. He said anyone who is in Christ is a new creation and that in this new creation, there is no superiority, only equality.

28 There is neither Jew nor Gentile, neither slave nor free, nor is there male and female, for you are all one in Christ Jesus. Galatians 3:28 (NIV)

Look carefully at the scriptures, you will realize that Paul abandoned every idea of superiority; Jews are not superior to Gentiles, slaves are not inferior to freeborn, and Males are not superior to females. All humanity is equal and one in Christ. With such a truth, he also abolished any division or partition between people and emphasized union and companionship. Husbands and wives must see each other as one instead of two different people with one superior and the other inferior.

True love unites and exemplifies equality but natural love or erotic love thinks more highly of self than others. Until men learn to relate with their wives as partners and not as inferiors, marriages will keep falling apart.

Nuggets

1. It is an evidence of lack of true love for a man to treat or relate with his wife as a slave.

2. A husband, who thinks that he is superior to his wife and that his decisions are supreme and must be accepted by his wife, is simply displaying his ignorance of what true love is and what it means to be united with his wife.

3. A woman is not a slave to her husband but a coheir or joint heir with him. You and your wife are partners not boss and slave. If you fail to honor your wife as a partner, your prayers will be hindered.

4. Marriages in which men relate with their wives as partners last longer and are more peaceful and joyful than those in which the man is in a struggle for

supremacy and treats his wife like a slave.

5. It is important to note that men and women are created in the image of God. It is impossible for the image of God in a man to be superior to the image of God in a woman.

6. If we want peaceful and joyful marriages, we must abandon the idea of supremacy and rather relate with each other as partners, coheirs and companions.

7. Husbands and wives must see each other as one instead of two different people with one superior and the other inferior.

8. True love unites and exemplifies equality but natural love or erotic love thinks more highly of self than others. Until men learn to relate with their wives as

partners and not as inferiors,
marriages will keep falling apart.

Chapter Nine

There is No Fear in Love

Chapter Nine
There is No Fear in Love

We have discussed in the previous chapters various characteristics of true love and how they act as the building blocks or foundation of a peaceful and long-lasting marriage.

In this chapter, we shall take a look at a few more characteristics of true love. Our focus will be on these three: love always protects, always trusts and always hopes.

Love Always Protects

One trait that is common to all of us humans and animals alike is the tendency to protect whatever we love. Because we love our lives, we do everything to protect it from danger, harm and disgrace. Why do people protect their money? It is because they love money. Why do people protect their Jewelries? It is because they love them.

Whatever you love you would protect. In the same vein, when you truly love someone, you would protect him or her.

When it comes to marriage, couples must learn to protect each other. This means that each person must care so much about the other person that he or she would be ready to do anything to protect him or her. Protection does not only have to do with shielding someone from physical danger or death but also from shame, disgrace, hunger, pain etc.

At one time God wanted to prove his love for his beloved nation Israel and he said the following words to them through the prophet Isaiah:

But now, this is what the Lord says—he who created you, Jacob, he who formed you, Israel: "Do not fear, for I have redeemed you; I have summoned you by name; you are mine.2 When you pass through the waters, I will be with you; and when you pass through the rivers, they will not sweep over you. When you walk through the fire, you will not be burned; the flames will not set you ablaze. 3 For I am the Lord your God, the Holy One of Israel, your Savior; I give Egypt for your ransom, Cush and Seba in your stead. 4 Since you are precious and honored in my sight, and because I love you, I will give people in exchange for you, nations in exchange for your life

Isaiah 43:1-4

From the verses above, we see God's love expressed in his protection for Israel. He told them not to be afraid that even though they go through water and fire, he would protect them and never allow the waters drown them or allow them get burned by the fire. God said he would do anything to preserve their lives; even if it means exchanging people and nations for their lives.

God knowing that Israel might not understand why he would go such a length to protect them, he decided to reveal the reason to them. He said ***"Since you are precious and honored in my sight, and because I love you"***. It is therefore obvious that the reason for all the protection and assurance is love; true love, Agape love.

This is the kind of love that every man must have for his wife; the love that protects from fire, waters, death, hunger, shame, disgrace, sicknesses and diseases. Every man must prove his love for his wife by protecting her from every angle and wherever he feels she is exposed.

 Men who humiliate their wives in public or before their in-laws cannot claim to love them. A real man will do everything possible to shield his wife from shame and disgrace. Same goes for the woman. A woman who loves her husband will shield him from shame and disgrace as long as it lies within her power to do so.

Women who love their husbands do not broadcast their faults or weaknesses in public or to outsiders. They rather help the man to become a better man in whatever way they can. All private discussions that could bring shame and disgrace are discussed in-house between husband and wife without bringing in a third party. The case is the same for men too. They must never wash their wives' dirty linen in public. All disputes should be settled privately and in love. True love will always protect!

There are a lot of irresponsible men in our societies today who do not protect their wives. Some fail to provide food and money for their wives thereby exposing them to hunger, shame and health challenges. One of the ways men can protect their wives is to always provide their needs. When a woman has all her needs met, she feels secured and protected in that marriage.

Love Always Trusts

One major challenge in marriages today is the issue of trust. Lack of trust is destroying most marriages today. Most women do not trust their husbands and most men do not trust their wives yet they claim to love each other. One of the characteristics of true love is that it always trusts. If the majority of marriages in our world today are void of trust, it is a proof that true love is grossly lacking in our world. I have seen marriages in which the man cannot access the woman's phone and the woman cannot access the man's phone. Both have secret passwords to their phones and have secret chats and messages they both hide from each other.

I have seen marriages in which the husbands suspect their wives and wives suspect their husbands. When it comes to money, most men cannot tell their wives the exact amount of money they earn as salaries neither do they tell their wives the password to their bank accounts. Most women even send spies to check on their husbands if they are actually at the office or if they branched elsewhere to see another woman. Whenever there is so much insecurity in a marriage, it is a sign that true love is absent in that marriage. No matter how many times we say "I love you" to our partners, if we cannot trust them, then that love is fake. True love is known by its ability to trust.

We do not need a minute-by-minute breakdown of where our beloved has been or what she or he has done because we trust them. -Andrew G. Marshall

Today, couples go into marriage with a signed prenuptial agreement; an agreement made by a couple before they marry concerning the ownership of their respective assets should the marriage fail. As good as this may seem, it is simply a proof that both parties are going into marriage with insecurity and lack of trust for each other. They are not sure if the marriage would last. They are already expecting a divorce before they had started the marriage process. Such fear of divorce in a marriage that has not even started indicates a huge lack of true love. True love is not afraid; it is full of trust and hope.

When couples suspect each other and do not feel saved in the marriage, it is a sign that true love is lacking in that marriage. True love always trusts and besides trusting, it always hopes for the best.

Love Always Hopes

Any marriage where there is fear and uncertainty is devoid of true love. There is no fear in love. Wherever there is perfect love fear varnishes. One of the hallmarks of true love is hope.

17 Love has been perfected among us in this: that we may have boldness in the Day of Judgment; because as He is, so are we in this world. 18 There is no fear in love; but perfect love casts out fear, because fear involves torment. But he who fears has not been made perfect in love. {1 John 4:17-18}

Unfortunately for most marriages today, there is fear of divorce and a feeling of insecurity. When two people who say they love each other are afraid of what will become of their marriage, it is a pointer to the fact that true love is lacking in that marriage. True love always hopes for the best and is not characterized by insecurity.

A major aspect of hope is seeing the best in your partner. When you truly love someone, you will always see the best in them. They may not be perfect at the moment and may never achieve perfection, but you keep seeing them for what they could become and not what they currently are. If couples can see the best in each other, then faults and weaknesses can easily be forgiven as both parties work on each other to become the best they could be.

"If we treat people as they are, we make them worse. If we treat people as they ought to be, we help them become what they are capable of becoming."

— Johann Wolfgang von Goethe

True love is always hopeful and believes in the ability of others to grow and become better. True love says "I know our marriage is not what it should be now, but we can work on ourselves to make it what it ought to be". When partners are full of hope, they do not envisage divorce, they hope for growth, maturity and everlasting love.

There is no fear in love! Perfect love casts out all fears!

Nuggets

1. Whatever you love you would protect. In the same vein, when you truly love someone, you would protect him or her. When it comes to marriage, couples must learn to protect each other.

2. Every man must prove his love for his wife by protecting her from every angle and wherever he feels she is exposed.

3. Women who love their husbands do not broadcast their faults or weaknesses in public or to outsiders. They rather help the man to become a better man in whatever way they can. All private discussions that could bring shame and disgrace are discussed in-house between husband and wife without bringing in a third party.

4. Whenever there is so much insecurity in a marriage, it is a sign that true love is absent in that marriage. No matter how

many times we say "I love you" to our partners, if we cannot trust them, then that love is fake. True love is known by its ability to trust.

5. Any marriage where there is fear and uncertainty is devoid of true love. There is no fear in love. Wherever there is perfect love fear varnishes.

6. If couples can see the best in each other, then faults and weaknesses can easily be forgiven as both parties work on each other to become the best they could be.

7. True love is always hopeful and believes in the ability of others to grow and become better. True love says "I know our marriage is not what it should be now, but we can work on ourselves to make it what it ought to be". When partners are full of hope, they do not envisage divorce, they hope for growth, maturity and everlasting love.

Chapter Ten

The Enemies of True Love

Chapter Ten
The Enemies of True Love

We have spent the last nine chapters of this book discussing what true love is and how to identify it. We have seen the 15 characteristics or seeds upon which true love thrives.

In this final chapter, I would like to bring to your notice that just as there are 15 seeds or characteristics of true love that keep marriages together, so are there 15 enemies of true love that keep marriages apart. These enemies of true love are traits of natural or human love. They are opposed to the nature of true love. These traits are impatience, unkindness, envy, boastfulness, pride, rudeness, selfishness, anger, Un-forgiveness and a host of others.

Impatience, Unkindness and Envy

Impatience: Without patience, it is difficult to start a relationship or walk in love. When you don't have the Spirit of Patience, you will also lack endurance and Godly love). Only people with true love can endure in marriages. God is love (1John 4:8) and he waited patiently with mankind for 120 years while Noah was building the Ark (1Peter 3:20). In the same vein husbands and wives can only have this kind of patience when they have the love of God. As we have already said in previous chapters, God is love and the first character of love is patience. Impatience in any marriage shows that there is no true love. It is an enemy of successful marriage. Impatience has destroyed so many marriages and good relationships than many other characters of human love that we will discuss below. If you allow impatience rule your marriage, it will ruin it.

2. Unkindness: No partner will want to remain in a relationship with someone who is harsh and cruel most of the time. Any marriage where there is no true love, there will be no joy, because kindness and joy are fruit of the Spirit, (Galatians 5:22-23). Unkindness in a marriage makes it difficult for husbands and wives to help one another, but where there is true love; they are kind to one another and help each other. You cannot say I love my wife or husband and be unkind to them. This is why marriages without true love foundations are full of sad stories. If you do not show kindness to your partner, your marriage will mostly end on a sad note.

3. Envy: This is one of the characters mentioned in the fifteen characters of true love, known as selfish jealousy where the husband or the wife has personal desires to increase personal possessions. The Bible says "Envy rots the bones" (Proverbs 14:30). Where there is true love, what the husband has belongs to the wife and verse versa. So, in marriages where there is no true love, there are no selfless services. Such a marriage is full of selfishness which is depicted by such languages as 'me, I and my'. Such languages do not exist in true love. Envy brings hatred into the relationship and is soon followed by a loss of intimacy. According to gotquestions.org, 'true love is God's love and God's love rejoices when others are blessed', but where there is no true love, husbands or wives only want to benefit themselves. They are never contented and the focus is always on them not on others. When envy thrives in a relationship, the days of that relationship are numbered. It will crash soon.

Boastfulness, Pride and Rudeness

4. Boastfulness: Another one of the negatives among the lists of what true love is not is boastfulness. Boastful people are braggarts who always talk about themselves, but true love is other – centered. Husbands and wives must always put the interest of their spouse before themselves. The language of I, mine, only exist in human – love, but the language of 'we' 'ours', are words found in true love marriages. There is no boasting in true love because true love is focused on the one being loved. There is no arrogance in true love because arrogance is twins of boasting.

5. Pride: The word pride can often replace boastfulness. A proud person thinks more of himself or herself. They are 'big headed' and inflate themselves and think more highly of themselves than they ought to. They think that everything must be about them; what they have achieved, who they are and what they can do. They look down on their partners and think so highly of themselves to the extent that they put their partners down. Prideful people always believe that their partners cannot do anything without them. Proud husbands or wives do not build homes but destroys homes as a result of their selfishness. They don't have true love in them at all. Prideful people cheat on their partner without remorse. Pride is one of the greatest enemies of true love and successful marriages.

6. Rudeness: This is also among the list of what true love is not in the fifteen characters of true love. Rude people are ill – mannered, selfish, and think that everything is about them. They belittle their partners in public and are uncivilized. In true love marriages there is no room for rudeness. Husbands and wives treat each other with gentleness and great respect. They understand that they both are one. When I am rude to my wife/husband, I am rude to myself and that means madness because only mad people scream and hit themselves. So when you are rude to your wife or husband, you are hurting yourself.

Selfishness, Anger, Un-forgiveness

7. Self – Seeking (Selfishness): selfishness is one of the foremost characters of the devil and it is the worst sin in marriage. In marriage husbands/wives should always put the other person first. Bing other-centered in marriage is the heart of true love. If true love is the foundation you are building your marriage on, the language of 'me man, and me woman, will be replaced with 'ours', because in true love marriages both partners are one. However, in human – love marriages, couples are two. Spouses are in for what they can get from the other person. There is no sacrifice. Selfishness is the order of the day in human-love marriages.

8. Anger: Uncontrolled anger has cost people so many valuable things in life; their marriages, jobs, relationships, friends, families, etc. and this is a sign of lack of true love. But with true love, you put your anger under control because the first character of true love is patience. Once you invite Jesus Christ into your heart, the fifteen characters of Truelove becomes yours instantly, in Romans 5:5 *"Now hope does not disappoint, because the love of God has been poured out in our hearts by the Holy Spirit who was given to us"*, the more we love Christ the more this love grow in us, because the Spirit now in us is the Spirit of Jesus Christ and the more we love our spouses also.

Note that true love in you empowers you to love others, and put others first before you. Human-love on the other hand is selfishness and puts self before others. 'I have to have my way all the time and when I don't get my way I get angry'. That is the nature of human love.

Human nature empowers anger but the Spirit of true love which comes from God empowers one to control his or her anger. This is why every couple needs to have the Spirit of true love in their heart. It is so important, because it affects every area of your life. Jesus' nature is love and the closer you are to Christ the more love you have and you can give to each other.

9 Keeping Records of Wrongs:

If you are in a relationship and cannot forget past wrongs, the relationship is on the death row. This normally happens in human -love marriages, where there is no true love foundation. No partner will tolerate past wrongs being re – run, re-played each time there is an argument or quarrel. Forgiveness is the greatest expression of true love, but un-forgiveness is deadly and poisonous to marriages and any relationship. In true love marriages, there is what is called "advance forgiveness"

In true love marriages; couples do not allow the sun to go down before they forgive one another. If you fail to forgive your spouse, you are like someone carrying a dead body while climbing a hill, the smell and all consequences that follow dead bodies are on you and that kills. So why not bury it and free yourself from the burden. The one that learn to forgive is the one that is free and lighter. Forgiveness comes easy when you have true love in your heart. Keeping record of wrongs is an enemy of love and successful marriage. .

Other Hindrances to True Love

10. Delighting In Evil Instead Of Rejoicing in the Truth:

Jesus says in the Bible, John 14:6 "I am the way, the truth and the Life". If Jesus is the truth and at the same time the true love, it means that in marriages where there is no true love, husbands and wives will always plan evil against each other.

They will hide money and embark on projects without the knowledge of the other person and all manner of evil will prevail in that marriage. But in true love marriages, truth is the watch Word. Partners with true love always agree on what to do because of the love they have for each other. In marriages where there is no truth, the couples hide even the human love they have from each other, due to hatred. They lie to one another, cheat on one another and love anything evil because there is no truth in them.

11. Lack of Protection:

In marriages not built on true love, husbands and wives find it difficult to protect the weaknesses of each other. However, where there is true love, the couples keep secrets of one another from outsiders. They know that husband and wife are one, so revealing the secrets of husband is same as revealing the secret of the wife.

The husbands are to protect their wives and not to physically abuse their wives. Any man that beats and abuses his wife does not love himself. He needs Jesus Christ (the Holy Spirit) in his heart. That means he needs the love of God (true love). Marriages where there is true love are void of domestic violence. The Husband's physical strength is there to also protect the wife from outside attack

12. Lack of Trusts (Mistrust)

Trust is one of the four specific actions that will always be performed by true love. True love (1).Trusts (2) Protects (3) Hopes (4) Perseveres, but in marriages were there are no true love you will not find the above characters.

Believe is another meaning of trust in the new standard version, NSV translation of the Bible. Our trust (believing) in God gives us the grace to trust (believe) in our husbands/wives. But that does not mean believers are naive or gullible. Human love is based on conditions. There is no sacrifice and husbands and wives are suspicious of one another. Trust only works in a household built on true love.

13. **Hopelessness:** In true love marriages, the couples always hope for the best. Remember that hope is the thirteenth character of Truelove. But the opposite is the case in human-love marriages (hopelessness), because there is no hope as the marriage progresses. In true love marriages, there is always hope. The Bible says in 1 John 4:8 "But anyone who does not love does not know God, for God is love".

In 1 Timothy 1:1 "Paul, an apostle of Christ Jesus by the command of God our savior and of Christ Jesus our hope", so this means that without Jesus Christ the foundation, the center of your marriage, is hopelessness. When Jesus Christ lives in us we have hope, but if not in us we are hopeless and the devil messes up our marriages.

14. Lack of Perseverance:

In the fifteen characters of true love, there are four actions that is "always" performs. The fourth one is love "always perseveres". This means that any marriage where there is true love, husbands and wives will always perseveres in the face of opposition, whether it is convenient or not, whether it is easy or not. Marriages were true love is the foundation, husbands and wives endure, remain, they don't quit. This is the meaning of the wedding vows, "for better or for worse, for richer, for poor, in sickness and in health, to love and to cherish; from this day forward until death do us part"

This vow only works in marriages built on truelove but in human-love marriages, this is only for wedding ceremony and not for the marriage. The marriage without true love finds it difficult to endure. It lacks perseverance in the face of opposition; therefore they quit their marriages easily. A good example is the Lord Jesus bearing with the church even though she messes up big time. True love loves the unlovable.

15. **Love Fails Easily**

The Bible says in 1 John 4:8 "He who does not love does not know God, for God is love", the fifteenth character of true love says Love never fails, but here we are told "love fails easily". The fifteen characters of human-love mentioned here, are also the Devil's characters, which are the opposite characters of true love. And these are the characters the enemy uses to destroy marriages, relationships. So you can see why human-love marriages fails easily, (they are built without foundations).

Note that God is love and God is Eternal, meaning everlasting, so you can see why marriages built with God (Truelove), as the foundation, and at the center never fails. God's kind of love (Truelove) never fails, it is forever and constant. God says in Jeremiah 31:3 "I have loved you with an everlasting love". Marriages fail when they are built on the wrong foundation of human love which is the enemy of true love.

I would love to encourage you to strive to emulate the love of Christ, which is selfless, sacrificial and everlasting if you want to enjoy peaceful and long lasting relationships. I do believe that you will imbibe the 15 seeds of true love that you have learned in this book into your life and marriage. I have no doubt that as you do, you would see the tremendous peace and joy that will prevail in your home. I therefore congratulate you in advance:

Do enjoy a heaven on earth marriage! Cheers!

CHOICE

TRUELOVE	HUMAN-LOVE
Is Patient	Impatient
Is Kind	Unkindness
Does not Envy	Full of Envy
Does not Boast	Boastfulness
Is not Proud	Full of Pride
Is not Rude	Rudeness
Is not self – seeking	Self Seeking
Is not easily Angered	Full of Anger
Keep no records of wrongs	Keeps record of wrongs
Does not delight in evil, but	Delights in evil instead of
Rejoices in the truth	rejoicing in the truth
Always Protect	Lack of Protection
Always Trust	Lack of Trust
Always Hopes	Hopelessness
Always Perseveres	Lack of Perseverance
Never Fails	High rate of failure

CHOICE

Do you know that every choice you make in life ends up choosing you? If you choose alcohol, alcohol will end up choosing you. If you choose truelove that becomes your believe system and your believe system determines your circumstances in life.

Now that you have choosing truelove, the circumstances in your marriage, and other relationships will be that truelove will be waxing stronger and stronger. If you choose human-love, the consequences will be full of emotional breakdown, high failure rates because it has no foundation, based on conditional love.

Are you tired of jumping from one marriage to another, from one relationship to another hoping it will work? Failed marriages left and right?, by choosing truelove disappointments in marriage failure will be a thing of the past. If you answer "yes" to truelove, then pray the following prayer and the Holy Spirit (Truelove) will come into your heart by faith. Your marriage and love- life will never fail, because truelove never fails.

PRAYER OF SALVATION

"O Lord God, I come to you in the name of Jesus Christ. Your word says, "…whoever calls on the name of the lord shall be saved" (Acts 2:21).
I ask Jesus to come into my heart to be the lord of my life. I receive eternal life into my spirit and according to Romans 10:9, "that if you confess with your mouth the lord Jesus and believe in your heart that God has raised Him from the dead, you will be saved, "I declare that I am saved; I am a child of God!

I now have Christ dwelling in me; greater is He that is in me than he that is in the world! (1 John 4:4), so I can boldly walk in love now!

Reference

Chapter Three
Love Never Fails

1. https://www.huffpost.com/entry/i-filed-for-divorce-3-months-after-wedding_n_5b5b6cc8e4b0de86f4970641

Chapter Four
The DNA of Real Love

1. How I ruined my marriage because of pride,https://www.nairaland.com/3099740/how-ruined-marriage-because-pride
2. https://www.kevinathompson.com/10-warning-signs-pride-marriage/

Chapter Six
The Real Picture of Love

1. Get the Facts & Figures, https://www.thehotline.org/resources/statistics/
2. Read more: https://www.legit.ng/836038-police-arraign-alleged-wife-killer-lekan-shonde-murder.html
3. Read more: https://www.legit.ng/1226364-court-sentences-nigerian-man-lekan-shonde-death-killing-wife.html

4.   Delhi: Man stabs wife to death, chops body into pieces,
https://www.indiatoday.in/crime/story/delhi-man-stabs-wife-to-death-chops-body-into-pieces-1601967-2019-09-22

Chapter Seven
Why Marriages Fail
1.   Marriage & divorce,
https://www.apa.org/topics/divorce/
2.   Bishop Noel Jones on Marriage!
https://theoldblackchurch.blogspot.com/2016/06/bishop-noel-jones-on-marriage.html

Chapter Eight
The Struggle for Supremacy
1.   https://www.amazon.com/AM-WOMAN-HUMAN-UNLEASHING-POTENTIAL-ebook/dp/B07LDGK7CT

About The Book

Our world is currently facing marital and relationship crisis in an unprecedented manner and rate. Every other day, there is a record of divorce, broken relationships and domestic violence. These menaces are not only happening in the underdeveloped 3rd world nations of the world but also in the highly developed 1st world nations like the United States of America and the United Kingdom. Divorce, marital crisis and domestic violence are a global issue. The author Gabriel Unaji, in this book, x-rays the problems and offers practical solutions to couples and partners who desire to enjoy peaceful and long-lasting marriages and relationship.

In this book you will learn:

1. The true definition and meaning of love

2. The four types of love and the role each plays in marriage

3. Why true love is eternal and why those who fall in love soon fall apart.

4. The DNA of true love and the 15 traits it codes for.

5. Why husbands should love their wives as Christ loved the church.

6. How submission and Domination have been abused in marriages.

7. Why marriages fail and divorce is gradually becoming a norm.

8. Why wives are not slaves and husbands not slave-masters.

9. Why there is no fear in love.

10. The 15 enemies of true love

About The Author

Mr. Gabriel Unaji - known as Dr of truelove is the founder of Truelovefoundation.com, a registered charity in the United Kingdom. He has a program called "truelove clinic" for the cure of all diseases in marriages with the 15 characters of truelove, and teaches couples how these characters form the foundational pillars for the building of marriages that will never fail. Gabriel is passionate about making sure no marriage fails due to lack of knowledge of true love. He holds a BA in theology from Canterbury Christ church University, Canterbury in United Kingdom and is presently pursuing a master's degree in theology at Roehampton University in London, United Kingdom.